Breakaway MATHS

Level 1
Teacher's Resource Book

Thomas Nelson and Sons Ltd
Nelson House Mayfield Road
Walton-on-Thames Surrey
KT12 5PL   UK

Thomas Nelson Australia
102 Dodds Street
South Melbourne
Victoria 3205 Australia

Nelson Canada
1120 Birchmount Road
Scarborough Ontario
MIK 5G4 Canada

First published by Thomas Nelson and Sons Ltd 1995
I(T)P Thomas Nelson is an International Thomson
Publishing Company
I(T)P is used under licence

ISBN 0-17-421696-3
NPN 9 8 7 6 5 4 3 2 1

The author and publishers would like to thank the
following for their valuable contributions when
advising on the draft versions of Breakaway Maths:

Elizabeth Byrne, *Senior Area Learning Support
Teacher, South Gloucestershire*

Alison Fairley, *Beech Lawn School, Hillsborough,
Northern Ireland*

David Holdstock and Anne Twells, *Walsall Learning
Support Service*

Gerald Morris, *The Castle School, Castleford,
West Yorkshire*

John Wright, *Field Lane Primary School, Brighouse,
West Yorkshire*

Thanks are also due to the illustrator Louise Hill, who
helped to devise the four main characters.

Printed in the E.U.

Contents

Preface

It is common to find that people who claim to have been 'hopeless' at mathematics in school use it very skilfully and thoughtfully in everyday life. They have devised their own methods of solving problems, and developed skills appropriate to their work or situation. Whilst problem solving in everyday life may be motivating, there are difficulties in bringing this type of motivation into the classroom through maths textbooks.

Mainstream mathematics schemes assume a steady learning progression, from simple numbers and facts to larger numbers and more complex ideas. For most children, the schemes can be tailored to suit their natural pace and development. However, any child may become 'stuck' on a particular aspect of mathematics or arithmetic. This may be because of illness, absence or a learning difficulty. Other children will consistently make slower progress than their peers.

Breakaway Maths is designed to provide a resource for children who are having problems with remembering facts and acquiring mathematical skills. These problems can arise at any time, but are most likely to be identified, and cause concern, between Years 2 and 3. For example, a child of 7 years old may still be counting inaccurately, forming numbers poorly, or unable to distinguish between addition and subtraction.

These children need time, confidence building and a sense of achievement in order to overcome their difficulties. *Breakaway Maths* allows children to revisit any area of mathematics with which they are having problems. This does not mean that they will be simply repeating work. The mathematics is presented in a variety of contexts, through textbooks, workbooks and copymasters.

Wherever possible, the mathematics has been related to everyday life, or situations with which children can identify. The characters' environments and interests reflect children's own. Every effort has been made to make the characters, illustrations and examples neutral in terms of age, so that children do not see the work as 'babyish'. The stories take them to places they would like to go to. The scheme avoids the stereotyping of characters and concentrates on their strengths, constantly highlighting what they can do rather than what they cannot.

An important consideration in writing *Breakaway Maths* has been that whilst children may be working at a relatively low level of mathematics, they are maturing in other ways. Many will be developing wide interests and practical skills. The scheme recognises this and aims to exploit it through model-making activities, games, investigations and problem solving.

Practical work should be at the heart of any mathematics programme, particularly one designed to help children with difficulties. The use of counters, cubes and base ten materials is essential to help children to model numbers and operations such as addition and subtraction. These materials should never be seen as being 'babyish', or associated with failure. Practical activities are perhaps more important than paper and pencil exercises in providing sound learning experiences in measuring, handling data and making patterns. The *Breakaway Maths* books should in no way replace these practical classroom activities; in fact, this Teacher's Resource Book suggests many more.

Above all, *Breakaway Maths* shows that mathematics can be an exciting and rewarding activity rather than a daunting, theoretical study. *Breakaway Maths* equips real children for real life.

The structure of Breakaway Maths

Breakaway Maths is led by the textbooks. Each book tells a story, and each page contains one main mathematical theme. However, everyday life can involve the use of all sorts of mathematical skills and present lots of information to decode, and so do the textbook pages.

If children have any problems with an aspect of the mathematics, or need to try it again to develop their confidence, they can go straight to the appropriate workbook. There are two workbooks corresponding to each textbook. The first one contains all the supporting number work such as sorting, counting, addition and subtraction. The second contains work on shape and space, measurement and handling data, although number work will be encountered here as well.

Children may require yet more practice, and this can be found in the copymaster book. This also contains materials for games, models and pattern making, and sheets to help children record their answers to questions on the textbook pages.

The diagram on the right shows how the components could fit together.

The idea is to give, to those children who need them, plenty of experiences of each mathematical theme, before moving them on to the next page in the textbook. However, it is not necessary to use every single page or component, as this can be just as frustrating as moving on too quickly. As always, the teacher's judgement is crucial.

The charts on pages 16 to 23 give a detailed description of the mathematical content of each textbook, and its links with the other materials.

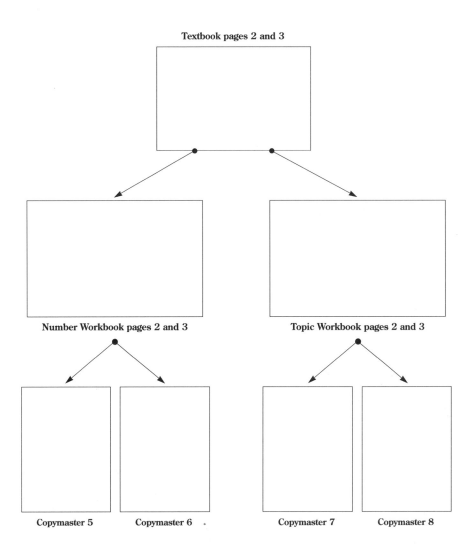

The Breakaway Maths materials

To provide the breadth and quantity of material to support children with special needs in mathematics, *Breakaway Maths* has four main components:

1 THE TEACHER'S RESOURCE BOOK

This book is intended to provide a guide to the materials, suggestions about their organisation, and links with the National Curriculum. It places mathematics in the context of everyday life, and gives ideas for practical work and activities. It also provides an answer key for the materials.

On pages 8 and 9, ways of organising are outlined, and links with the National Curriculum (for England and Wales, Scotland and Northern Ireland) are presented on pages 10 to 15.

Pages 16 to 23 show how the content of each textbook links to all the other materials. These pages may be photocopied and used as record sheets.

On pages 24 to 79, each double-page spread from the textbooks is taken in turn; there is a synopsis of the story, and the links between the textbook pages, the workbook pages and the copymasters are explained. There are suggestions for discussions, and some examples of the mathematics to look for in the school. Games and activities are also suggested. These either use readily available classroom equipment, or can be made from the copymasters. They can be used before or after the printed materials.

The answer key for all the pupil materials begins on page 80. This can be used either by teachers or by children who can check their own work.

At the back of the book, lists of key vocabulary show the restricted general vocabulary used in the textbooks, and the specialised language of mathematics which is systematically introduced.

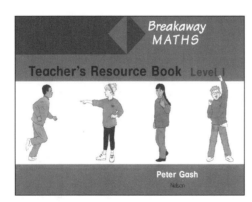

2 THE TEXTBOOKS

There are four textbooks at Level 1. They should be read in sequence.

The textbooks introduce the characters, Rupa, Lisa, David and Nicky. They describe the situations in which they find themselves, and invite children to help them solve problems.

Each textbook offers a self-contained story.

Book 1 introduces the characters and takes them to school, with lots of distractions along the way. They arrive just in time to go on a school trip. Book 2 describes the journey, a break for lunch, and arrival at their destination. Book 3 is based at the castle they are visiting. They have to complete their tasks, but still find time to enjoy themselves. Book 4 shows their journey home, and takes them back to school.

The text has been kept to a minimum with picture clues, plenty of repetition and very simple sentence structures. (See page 96 for vocabulary lists.)

At the foot of each page there are references to the other materials (workbooks and copymasters) which relate to the mathematical content of that page. This is to make the provision of extra practice as straightforward as possible.

The mathematical skills featured in the work on that page are also listed here. It is suggested that children move from a textbook page to those workbook pages which support it. If further work, for practice or enrichment, is needed, there are extra copymaster worksheets.

3 THE WORKBOOKS

For each textbook there are two workbooks, a Number Workbook and a Topic Workbook.

The Number Workbook provides more opportunities to develop and practise number skills.

The Topic Workbook provides further experiences of algebra, shape and space and handling data.

Each double-page spread in the workbooks corresponds to a single textbook page. The workbook pages present the same mathematical concepts as the associated textbook pages. Wherever possible, they also use some of the characters, or an aspect of the story, from the textbook. This can help children to recognise that they are already familiar with the kinds of problem being presented.

The workbooks provide an opportunity to revisit a mathematical theme and they allow teachers to show children some more applications of mathematics in everyday life. For example, children may read, write and order numbers up to 10 on doors, a telephone keypad, a calculator and a television handset, as well as on number lines and tracks.

On page 16 of each workbook there is a simple review of some of its contents. It is entitled 'I can ...', to give parents and children an indication of what has been covered. It can be signed by the teacher, the child, or both. It is not intended to be a formal assessment.

The note at the foot of every workbook page summarise the mathematical skills which have been practised. There are also references to the textbook pages and the associated copymasters.

4 THE COPYMASTERS

Copymasters may be used before, after or alongside the textbooks and workbooks.

Most of the worksheets provide more materials for the purpose of revisiting particular mathematical themes.

The pro-forma worksheets provide skeleton formats of activities which will be familiar to children who have already used the workbooks and copymaster worksheets.

The answer sheets provide formats for children to record their answers to questions in the textbook.

Some worksheets provide templates for making games and models and for pattern making. They offer children the opportunity to cut, paste and choose colours, and achieve a satisfying result.

Certificates to mark the completion of each textbook are also included. These are intended to give children a sense of achievement and a record of their progress.

An advantage of photocopying is that sheets can be modified to meet particular needs. When a copy has been made, correction fluid or 'post it' notes can be used to mask areas to leave space for teachers to write their own numbers, questions or instructions. It is always worth keeping a clean copy of any modified worksheet, to avoid having to repeat the task. Enlarging the photocopies can also help children, by giving them more space or making the images clearer. Some of the sheets can be turned into board games in this way.

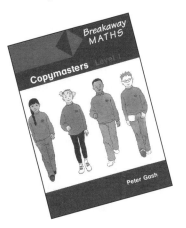

Classroom organisation

Classroom organisation

The most common ways in which children are organised to work on mathematics are individually, in pairs or in groups.

WORKING INDIVIDUALLY

A child is given a textbook, workbook or worksheet and asked to solve a series of problems. *Breakaway Maths* provides all these components at different levels, so that if the children are organised to work individually, those with difficulties can be using materials which look the same as those being used by the rest of the class. In this way they can avoid being perceived as doing special work.

In this situation, some children may have difficulty in reading the instructions in some texts. Long, involved instructions do not feature in *Breakaway Maths*, so that teachers, or other children, can quickly explain what the task is. The repetition of phrases and the picture clues will give the child the opportunity to work with a degree of independence.

WORKING IN PAIRS

Children with similar problems can be encouraged to work together on a particular set of problems, or a topic such as 2D shapes. The great advantage of this kind of classroom organisation is that it gives children the opportunity to discuss their difficulties and suggest solutions to each other. They can share the ownership of the work, which may help to build their confidence.

The investigations, problems and practical activities in *Breakaway Maths* are ideal vehicles for working in this way. The teacher's notes also suggest several games which are ideally played in pairs. Once these have been learned, children can play them repeatedly, and modify them by altering the range of cards or numbers used. In this way, they do not need to learn a new game in order to extend their use of mathematics.

WORKING IN GROUPS

All sorts of problems, particularly mathematical ones, can be very daunting if they have to be solved alone. Using teamwork is now an accepted way of addressing problems in an ever more complex world.

Similar ability groups

This is where a group of four to six children work together because they have similar abilities or problem areas, and it is more economical to introduce a body of work to them all. An example might be a group of children who do not understand the process of subtraction.

The teacher introduces the topic, showing how to use cubes to model subtraction problems. The children are then left to work on some examples together. In this way, they have all seen and heard what to do, and can help each other with any misunderstandings or difficulties. They can also be encouraged to check each other's work.

A session with such a group can be finished off with a simple game which uses the skill they have been developing. Alternatively, they can report back on what they have done.

Mixed ability groups

Pupils experiencing difficulties with aspects of mathematics need not be deprived of the chance to work with more able pupils. There are many practical problem-solving situations where children of different abilities can contribute to the solution.

The work in *Breakaway Maths* on building the housing estate and the castle is a good example of work suitable for a group of children with different abilities. These problems are open-ended in that there is no right answer, but rather a range of good, satisfactory or bad results. All the children can contribute by suggesting different approaches. The great advantage is that they will talk about what they are doing, and gain many incidental mathematical experiences.

Withdrawal groups

In some situations, children will be withdrawn from the classroom for a short period. This is more common for language work than mathematics. *Breakaway Maths* provides all the materials and structure needed to plan a programme for such groups.

The textbooks each provide a storyline which can be the stimulus for a session – 'I wonder what the children will do next time?' The workbooks and copymasters give plenty of scope for written work and recording. The games in the Teacher's Resource Book can be learned in withdrawal groups, for use back in the classroom.

Alternatively, teachers may wish to focus on one aspect of mathematics – such as naming, sorting and drawing 2D shapes – in this situation. In this case, they can use the problems on a particular textbook page to introduce the work. Children can then use the related pages in the Topic Workbook to continue the work. There will also be related copymasters, and ideas for further practical work in the Teacher's Resource Book.

HOW TO USE THE MATERIALS

The simplest way to use *Breakaway Maths* is for each child to begin with the textbook.

If the children are not using exercise books, each child will need to keep his/her own answer sheets. These will need to be photocopied in advance.

The textbooks provide a starting point. A highly structured approach is not essential, as any pages children can do easily will give them confidence. However, the textbooks are designed so that they can also be used in a structured way.

If children succeed on a page, they can simply continue through the textbook. The content increases in difficulty very gradually. However, to build confidence and a sense of achievement, they can revisit the mathematics on the appropriate workbook pages. References to these are at the foot of each textbook page. Workbooks are very useful, particularly if children experience difficulty with any of the material in the textbook. Workbooks hold the children's interest in work which they are beginning to understand. The copymasters also provide appropriate games and activities which reflect the content of the textbooks.

When children and teachers are confident to move on, they can turn to the next textbook page and all its associated materials. However, the textbooks regularly revisit topics so that children can build steadily on their success.

This is only one model for using the materials. Teachers may wish to concentrate on all the workbook pages about a particular subject, such as counting to 10, and then follow up with the copymasters. *Breakaway Maths* is a flexible resource which can support individual ways of organising the materials.

Breakaway Maths and the National Curriculum

ENGLAND AND WALES Mathematics in the National Curriculum (1995)

The National Curriculum Programmes of Study for Key Stage 1 have informed the textbooks, workbooks and copymasters for Level 1. The skills described in 'Using and applying mathematics' underpin all the materials, and references to these are not included in this chart.

			NUMBER	SHAPE, SPACE AND MEASURES
Textbook 1				
Pages	2–5	Counting to 5	2ab	
		Reading digital and analogue time		4a
	6	Numerals to 10	2ab	
	7	Identifying 2D shapes	5a	2a
	8–9	Planning routes		3a
	10	Language of position		3a
	11	Continuing patterns	3a	2a
	12	Identifying 3D shapes	5a	2a
		Language of position		3a
	13	Ordering numbers to 10	2ab	
	14	Language of position		3a
	15	Addition to 10	2ab, 3bd, 4a	

			NUMBER	SHAPE, SPACE AND MEASURES
Textbook 2				
Pages	2–3	Counting to 10	2ab	
	4	Addition to 10	3bd, 4a	
	5	Subtraction from 10	3bd, 4a	
	6	Identifying 2D shapes	5a	2a
	7	Language of direction		3a, 4a
	8	Addition to 10	2ab, 3bd, 5a	
	9	Subtraction from 10	2ab, 3bd, 4a	
	10	Identifying 3D shapes	5a	2a
	11	Addition to 10	3bd, 4a, 5a	
	12	Language of position		3a
	13	Language of measurement		4a
	14	Copying patterns	3a	2a, 4a
	15	Identifying 3D shapes	5a	2ab

			NUMBER	SHAPE, SPACE AND MEASURES
Textbook 3				
Page	2	Counting to 10	2ab, 5a	
		Reading analogue time		4a
	3	Identifying 2D shapes	5a	2ab
	4	Counting to 10	2ab, 3bd, 5a	
	5	Analogue time		4a
		Roman numerals	3a	
	6	Number patterns to 10	2ab, 3a	2a
	7	Counting up, counting down	3bd, 4a	
	8	Language of position		3a
		Language of measurement		4a
	9	Language of position		3a
	10	Identifying 3D shapes	5a	2a
	11	Growing number patterns	3a	
	12	Addition to 10	2ab, 3bd, 4a	3a
	13	Language of position		3a
		Counting to 10	2ab	
		Reading analogue time		4a
	14–15	Using money to 10p	2ab, 3bd, 4a	

			NUMBER	SHAPE, SPACE AND MEASURES
Textbook 4				
Page	2	Addition to 10	2ab, 3bd, 5a	
	3	Identifying 3D shapes	5a	2a
		Reading analogue time		4a
	4	Language of measurement		4a
		Reading analogue time		4a
	5	Language of position		3a
		Language of measurement		4a
	6	Counting on (using a number line)	3bd, 4ac	

	NUMBER	SHAPE, SPACE AND MEASURES
Textbook 4 *(cont.)*		
Page 7 Continuing patterns	3a	2a
8–9 Addition to 10 Reading analogue time	3bd, 4ac	3a 4a
10–11 Larger than, smaller than	2ab, 4c	
12 Language of position	2ab	3a
13 Counting to 10 Addition to 10	2ab, 5a 3bd, 4ac	
14 Numbers of sides of 2D shapes		2ac
15 Language of position Reading analogue time		3a 4a

Many pages in *Breakaway Maths* cover more than one area of mathematics, as defined by the National Curriculum Programmes of Study. This chart is to help teachers who wish to find pages in the textbooks with an emphasis on a particular area of mathematics. 'Opportunities' described in 'Number 1' and 'Shape, space and measures 1' pervade the whole scheme, and are especially emphasised in this book.

	Textbook 1 pages	*Textbook 2 pages*	*Textbook 3 pages*	*Textbook 4 pages*
NUMBER				
2 Developing an understanding of place value	2–6, 13, 15	2, 8, 9	2, 4, 6, 12–15	2, 10–13
3 Understanding relationships between numbers and developing methods of computation	15	4, 5, 8, 9, 11, 14	4–7, 11, 12, 14, 15	2, 6–8, 13
4 Solving numerical problems	15	4, 5, 9, 11	7, 12, 14, 15	6, 8–11, 13
5 Classifying, representing and interpreting data	7, 12	6, 8, 10, 11	2–4, 10	2, 13
SHAPE, SPACE AND MEASURES				
2 Understanding and using patterns and properties of shape	7, 11, 12	6, 10, 14, 15	3, 6, 10	3, 7, 14
3 Understanding and using patterns and properties of position and movement	8–10, 12, 14	7, 12	8, 9, 12, 13	5, 8, 9, 12, 15
4 Understanding and using measures	4, 5	7, 13, 14	2, 5, 8, 13	3–5, 8, 9, 15

Breakaway Maths and the 5–14 Guidelines

SCOTLAND   The Scottish Office Education Department: Mathematics 5–14 Guidelines

The Scottish National Curriculum strands have informed the textbooks, workbooks and copymasters. The 'Handling information' strands Collect A and Interpret A underpin all the work, as children can gain all the necessary information from the pictures and diagrams in *Breakaway Maths*. These are not included in this chart.

Textbook 1

Pages		HANDLING INFORMATION	NUMBER, MONEY AND MEASUREMENT	SHAPE, POSITION AND MOVEMENT
2–5	Counting to 5 Reading digital and analogue time	Organise A	Range and type of numbers A Time A	
6	Numerals to 10	Organise A	Range and type of numbers A	
7	Identifying 2D shapes	Organise A		Range of shapes A
8–9	Planning routes	Display A		Position and movement A
10	Language of position			Position and movement A
11	Continuing patterns	Display A	Patterns and sequences A	
12	Identifying 3D shapes Language of position	Organise A		Range of shapes A Position and movement A
13	Ordering numbers to 10	Organise A	Range and type of numbers A	
14	Language of position	Organise A	Range and type of numbers A	
15	Addition to 10		Add and subtract A	

Textbook 2

Pages		HANDLING INFORMATION	NUMBER, MONEY AND MEASUREMENT	SHAPE, POSITION AND MOVEMENT
2–3	Counting to 10	Organise A	Range and type of numbers A	
4	Addition to 10	Organise A	Range and type of numbers A	
5	Subtraction from 10	Organise A	Add and subtract A	
6	Identifying 2D shapes	Display A		Range of shapes A
7	Language of direction			Position and movement A
8	Addition to 10		Add and subtract A	
9	Subtraction from 10		Add and subtract A	
10	Identifying 3D shapes	Display A		Range of shapes A
11	Addition to 10		Add and subtract A	
12	Language of position	Display A		Position and movement A
13	Language of measurement		Measure and estimate A	
14	Copying patterns	Display A	Patterns and sequences A	
15	Identifying 3D shapes	Organise A Display A		Range of shapes A

Textbook 3

Pages		HANDLING INFORMATION	NUMBER, MONEY AND MEASUREMENT	SHAPE, POSITION AND MOVEMENT
2	Counting to 10 Reading analogue time	Display A	Range and type of numbers A Time A	
3	Identifying 2D shapes	Display A		Range of shapes A
4	Counting to 10	Organise A	Range and type of numbers A	
5	Analogue time Roman numerals	Organise A Display A	Patterns and sequences A Time A	
6	Number patterns to 10	Organise A	Patterns and sequences A	
7	Counting up, counting down	Organise A	Patterns and sequences A	
8	Language of position Language of measurement	Display A	Measure and estimate A	
9	Language of position			Position and movement A
10	Identifing 3D shapes	Display A		Range of shapes A
11	Growing number patterns	Display A	Patterns and sequences A	
12	Addition to 10		Add and subtract A	
13	Language of position Counting to 10 Reading analogue time		Range and type of numbers A Time A	Position and movement A
14–15	Using money to 10p		Money A Add and subtract A	

Textbook 4

Page		HANDLING INFORMATION	NUMBER, MONEY AND MEASUREMENT	SHAPE, POSITION AND MOVEMENT
2	Addition to 10	Organise A	Add and subtract A	
3	Identifying 3D shapes Reading analogue time	Organise A	Time A	Range of shapes A
4	Language of measurement Reading analogue time	Organise A	Measure and estimate A Time A	
5	Language of position Language of measurement	Display A	Measure and estimate A	Position and movement A
6	Counting on (using a number line)		Add and subtract A	
7	Continuing patterns	Display A	Patterns and sequences A	
8–9	Addition to 10 Reading analogue time		Add and subtract A Time A	
10–11	Larger than, smaller than	Organise A	Add and subtract A	
12	Language of position			Position and movement A
13	Counting to 10 Addition to 10	Display A Organise A	Range and type of numbers A Add and subtract A	
14	Numbers of sides of 2D shapes	Display A		Range of shapes A
15	Language of position Reading analogue time		Time A	Position and movement A

Many pages in *Breakaway Maths* cover more than one area of mathematics as defined by the National Curriculum.
This chart is to help teachers who wish to find pages in the textbooks with an emphasis on a particular strand.

	Textbook 1 pages	Textbook 2 pages	Textbook 3 pages	Textbook 4 pages
HANDLING INFORMATION				
Strands				
Collect A	Children obtain information from all the pictures in the textbooks.			
Organise A	2–7, 12–14	2–5, 15	4–7	2–4, 10, 11, 13
Display A	8, 9, 11	6, 10, 12, 14, 15	2, 3, 5, 8, 10, 11	5, 7, 14
Interpret A	Children have to interpret the illustrations in all the textbooks.			
NUMBER, MONEY AND MEASUREMENT				
Strands				
Range and type of numbers	2–6, 13, 14	2, 3	2, 4, 13	
Money			14, 15	
Addition and subtraction	15	4, 5, 8, 9, 11	12, 14, 15	2, 6, 8, 10, 11, 13
Patterns and sequences	11	14	5, 6, 7, 11	7
Measurement and estimation		13	8	4, 5
Time	2–5, 8		2, 5, 13	4, 9, 15
SHAPE, POSITION AND MOVEMENT				
Strands				
Range of shapes	7, 12	6, 10, 15	3, 10	3, 14
Position and movement	8–10, 12	7, 12	9	5, 12, 15

Breakaway Maths and the Northern Ireland Curriculum

NORTHERN IRELAND   **Department of Education for Northern Ireland:**
Mathematics Programmes of Study and Attainment Targets

The Northern Ireland National Curriculum Attainment Targets have informed the textbooks, workbooks and copymasters. The use of materials and talking about work, as described in 'Processes in mathematics (P1)', underpin all the work in *Breakaway Maths*, and references to these are not included in this chart.

Textbook 1

Pages

	NUMBER	ALGEBRA	MEASURES	SHAPE AND SPACE	HANDLING DATA
2–5 Counting to 5 Reading digital and analogue time	N/1a				
6 Numerals to 10	N/1a				
7 Identifying 2D shapes				S/1b	D/1a
8–9 Planning routes				S/1d	
10 Language of position				S/1cd	
11 Continuing patterns		A/1			
12 Identifying 3D shapes Language of position				S/1bcd	D/1ab
13 Ordering numbers to 10	N/1a				
14 Language of position	N/1a				
15 Addition to 10	N/1ade				

Textbook 2

Pages

	NUMBER	ALGEBRA	MEASURES	SHAPE AND SPACE	HANDLING DATA
2–3 Counting to 10	N/1a				
4 Addition to 10	N/1ade				
5 Subtraction from 10	N/1ade				
6 Identifying 2D shapes				S/1b	D/1a
7 Language of direction				S/1cd	
8 Addition to 10	N/1ade				
9 Subtraction from 10	N/1ade				
10 Identifying 3D shapes				S/1b	D/1ab
11 Addition to 10	N/1ad				
12 Language of position				S/1cd	
13 Language of measurement			M/1		
14 Copying patterns		A/1			
15 Identifying 3D shapes				S/1ab	D/1a

Textbook 3

Page

	NUMBER	ALGEBRA	MEASURES	SHAPE AND SPACE	HANDLING DATA
2 Counting to 10 Reading analogue time	N/1a				D/1c
3 Identifying 2D shapes				S/1ab	D/1a
4 Counting to 10	N/1a				D/1a
5 Analogue time Roman numerals	N/1c	A/1			
6 Number patterns to 10	N/1a	A/1			
7 Counting up, counting down	N/1ad				
8 Language of position Language of measurement			M/1	S/1c	D/1b
9 Language of position				S/1cd	
10 Identifying 3D shapes				S/1b	D/1ac
11 Growing number patterns	N/1a	A/1			
12 Addition to 10	N/1ade				
13 Language of position Counting to 10 Reading analogue time	N/1a				
14–15 Using money to 10p	N/1acde		M/2b		

Textbook 4

Page

	NUMBER	ALGEBRA	MEASURES	SHAPE AND SPACE	HANDLING DATA
2 Addition to 10	N/1ad				D/1ab
3 Identifying 3D shapes Reading analogue time				S/1b	D/1a
4 Language of measurement Reading analogue time			M/1		
5 Language of position Language of measurement			M/1		
6 Counting on (using a number line)	N/1a				
7 Continuing patterns		A/1			
8–9 Addition to 10 Reading analogue time	N/1acde				
10–11 Larger than, smaller than	N/1acde				
12 Language of position				S/1cd	
13 Counting to 10 Addition to 10	N/1a				D/1a
14 Numbers of sides of 2D shapes				S/1ab	D/1a
15 Language of position				S/1cd	

Many pages in *Breakaway Maths* cover more than one area of mathematics as defined by the National Curriculum.
This chart is to help teachers who wish to find pages in the textbooks with an emphasis on a particular area of mathematics.

	Textbook 1 pages	Textbook 2 pages	Textbook 3 pages	Textbook 4 pages
NUMBER (N/1)	2–6, 13–15	2–5	8, 9, 11	2, 4–7, 11–15
ALGEBRA (A/1)	11	14	5, 6, 11	7
MEASURES (M/1)		13	7, 14, 15	7
SHAPE AND SPACE (S/1)	7–10, 12	6, 7, 10, 12, 15	3, 9, 10	3, 12, 14, 15
HANDLING DATA (D/1)	7, 12	6, 10, 15	2–4, 8, 10	2, 3, 13, 14

Pathways through the materials/record sheets

Textbook 1 – Late!

✓ Pages 16–23 may be photocopied and used as individual record sheets.

TEXTBOOK 1 PAGES

2	Counting to 5	☐
3	Counting to 5	☐
4	Counting to 5, reading analogue time	☐
5	Counting to 5, reading digital time	☐
6	Numerals to 10	☐
7	Identifying 2D shapes	☐
8	Planning routes	☐
9	Planning routes	☐
10	Language of position	☐
11	Continuing patterns	☐
12	Identifying 3D shapes, language of position	☐
13	Ordering numbers to 10	☐
14	Language of position	☐
15	Addition to 10	☐

COPYMASTERS (ANSWER SHEETS)

1	Textbook 1 Late! pages 2 to 5
2	Textbook 1 Late! pages 6 to 9
3	Textbook 1 Late! pages 10 to 11
4	Textbook 1 Late! pages 12 to 15

NUMBER WORKBOOK 1 PAGES

2 Counting to 10, writing numerals to 10 ☐
3 Reading number words to 10, writing numerals to 10 ☐

4 Counting to 10, writing numerals to 10 ☐
5 Reading number words to 10, writing numerals to 10 ☐

6 Counting to 10 ☐
7 More ☐

8 Counting to 10, writing numerals to 10 ☐
9 Fewer ☐

10 Ordering numbers to 10, writing numerals to 10 ☐
11 Ordering numbers to 10, writing numerals to 10 ☐

12 Ordering numbers to 10, writing numerals to 10 ☐
13 Ordering numbers to 10, writing numerals to 10 ☐

14 Addition to 10 ☐
15 Addition to 10 ☐

COPYMASTERS

5 Rupa's homework – counting ☐
6 Lisa's homework – counting ☐
7 David's breakfast – counting ☐
10 Nicky's computer – counting ☐

13 Build a housing estate – cut and paste ☐
14 Numeral cards to 10 – cut and paste ☐
17 Writing door numbers ☐

25 Number spot cards – cut and paste ☐
26 Ordering numbers ☐

27 Number facts ☐
28 Number facts ☐
29 Number facts ☐
30 Number facts ☐
31 Number facts ☐
32 Number facts ☐

TOPIC WORKBOOK 1 PAGES

2 Showing analogue time ☐
3 Reading analogue time ☐

4 Showing digital time ☐
5 Reading digital time ☐

6 Identifying 2D shapes ☐
7 Identifying 2D shapes ☐

8 Following directions ☐
9 Following directions ☐

10 Language of position ☐
11 Language of position ☐

12 Continuing patterns ☐
13 Continuing patterns ☐

14 Identifying 3D shapes ☐
15 Identifying 3D shapes ☐

COPYMASTERS

8 Digital time ☐
9 Blank digital clocks ☐

11 Analogue time ☐
12 Blank analogue clocks ☐

15 2D shape cards – cut and paste ☐
16 Drawing 2D shapes ☐

18 Map of Polygon Park ☐
19 Rectangular maze ☐
20 Curved maze ☐

21 Pattern cards – cut and paste ☐
22 Patterns to finish ☐

23 3D shape cards – cut and paste ☐
24 Naming 3D shapes ☐

Textbook 2 – On the bus

TEXTBOOK 2 PAGES

2 Counting to 10 ☐

3 Counting to 10 ☐

4 Addition to 10 ☐

5 Subtraction from 10 ☐

6 Identifying 2D shapes ☐

7 Language of direction ☐

8 Addition to 10 ☐

9 Subtraction from 10 ☐

10 Identifying 3D shapes ☐

11 Addition to 10 ☐

12 Language of position ☐

13 Language of measurement ☐

14 Copying patterns ☐

15 Identifying 3D shapes ☐

COPYMASTERS (ANSWER SHEETS)

33 Textbook 2 On the bus pages 2 to 5

34 Textbook 2 On the bus pages 6 to 9

35 Textbook 2 On the bus pages 10 to 13

36 Textbook 2 On the bus pages 14 to 15

NUMBER WORKBOOK 2 PAGES

2	Counting to 10, writing numerals to 10	☐
3	Counting to 10, writing numerals to 10	☐
4	The same as	☐
5	Counting to 10, writing numerals to 10	☐
6	Addition to 10	☐
7	Addition to 10	☐
8	Subtraction from 10	☐
9	Fewer	☐
10	Addition to 10	☐
11	Addition to 10	☐
12	Subtraction from 10	☐
13	Subtraction from 10	☐
14	Addition to 10	☐
15	Subtraction from 10	☐

COPYMASTERS

37	Buses – counting	☐
38	Train windows – the same	☐
39	Drawing more people	☐
40	Drawing more coats and pegs, subtraction from 10	☐
41	Addition	☐
42	Addition	☐
43	Subtraction	☐
44	Fewer	☐
49	Addition	☐
50	Addition	☐
51	Subtraction	☐
52	Addition and subtraction game cards – cut and paste	☐
55	Addition	☐
56	Subtraction	☐

TOPIC WORKBOOK 2 PAGES

2	Identifying 2D shapes	☐
3	Identifying 2D shapes, drawing 2D shapes	☐
4	Following directions	☐
5	Language of position	☐
6	Identifying 3D shapes	☐
7	Drawing 3D shapes	☐
8	Language of position	☐
9	Language of position	☐
10	Language of measurement	☐
11	Language of measurement	☐
12	Continuing patterns	☐
13	Continuing patterns	☐
14	Identifying 3D shapes	☐
15	Drawing 2D shapes	☐

COPYMASTERS

45	2D shape cards – cut and paste	☐
46	Drawing 2D shapes	☐
47	Following directions	☐
48	Following directions	☐
53	Matching 3D shapes	☐
54	Straight, curved, pointed, round	☐
57	Language of position	☐
58	Language of position cards – cut and paste	☐
59	Language of measurement	☐
60	Language of measurement	☐
61	Brick cards – cut and paste	☐
62	Brick patterns	☐
63	Make the castle (1)	☐
64	Make the castle (2)	☐

Textbook 3 – At the castle

TEXTBOOK 3 PAGES

2	Counting to 10, reading analogue time	☐
3	Identifying 2D shapes	☐
4	Counting to 10	☐
5	Analogue time, Roman numerals	☐
6	Number patterns to 10	☐
7	Counting up, counting down	☐
8	Language of position, language of measurement	☐
9	Language of position	☐
10	Identifying 3D shapes	☐
11	Growing number patterns	☐
12	Addition to 10	☐
13	Language of position, counting to 10, reading analogue time	☐
14	Using money to 10p	☐
15	Using money to 10p	☐

COPYMASTERS (ANSWER SHEETS)

65	Textbook 3 At the castle pages 2 to 4
66	Textbook 3 At the castle pages 5 to 6
67	Textbook 3 At the castle page 7
68	Textbook 3 At the castle pages 8 to 9
69	Textbook 3 At the castle pages 10 to 12
70	Textbook 3 At the castle pages 13 to 15

NUMBER WORKBOOK 3 PAGES

2 Mapping
3 Counting to 10

4 Counting to 10
5 Counting to 10

6 Decoding Roman numerals
7 Arrangements of numbers to 10

8 Counting up
9 Counting down

10 Addition to 10
11 Addition and subtraction to/from 10

12 Addition of money to 5p
13 Subtraction of money from 5p

14 Addition of money to 10p
15 Subtraction of money from 10p

COPYMASTERS

71 Mapping
72 Mapping

75 Drawing and counting

76 Number arrangements
77 Number patterns

80 Number line addition
81 Number line subtraction

89 Addition
90 Subtraction

93 Addition of money
94 Giving change

95 Coin cards – cut and paste

96 Price tag cards – cut and paste

TOPIC WORKBOOK 3 PAGES

2 Identifying 2D shapes
3 Drawing 2D shapes

4 Number patterns
5 Number patterns

6 Language of position
7 Language of measurement

8 Language of position
9 Language of position

10 Identifying 3D shapes
11 Drawing 3D shapes

12 Growing number patterns
13 Growing number patterns

14 Reading analogue time
15 Showing analogue time

COPYMASTERS

73 Patterns with 2D shapes
74 Drawings with 2D shapes

78 Number patterns
79 Number patterns

82 Language of position
83 Language of measurement cards – cut and paste

84 Language of position
85 Positioning 2D shapes

86 Drawing 3D shapes

87 Triangular numbers
88 Number patterns

91 Analogue time
92 Analogue time

Textbook 4 – Goodbye to the castle

TEXTBOOK 4 PAGES

2	Addition to 10	☐
3	Identifying 3D shapes, reading analogue time	☐
4	Language of measurement, reading analogue time	☐
5	Language of position, language of measurement	☐
6	Counting on (using a number line)	☐
7	Continuing patterns	☐
8	Addition to 10	☐
9	Addition to 10, reading analogue time	☐
10	Larger than	☐
11	Larger than, smaller than	☐
12	Language of position	☐
13	Counting to 10, addition to 10	☐
14	Numbers of sides of 2D shapes	☐
15	Language of position, reading analogue time	☐

COPYMASTERS (ANSWER SHEETS)

97	Textbook 4 Goodbye to the castle pages 2 to 5
98	Textbook 4 Goodbye to the castle pages 6 to 7
99	Textbook 4 Goodbye to the castle pages 8 to 11
100	Textbook 4 Goodbye to the castle pages 12 to 15

NUMBER WORKBOOK 4 PAGES

2	Counting to 10	☐
3	Counting to 10 using twos	☐
4	Counting on (using number lines)	☐
5	Counting back (using number lines)	☐
6	Addition to 10	☐
7	Addition to 10	☐
8	Counting to 10	☐
9	Counting to 10, addition to 10	☐
10	Missing numbers to 5	☐
11	Missing numbers to 10	☐
12	Missing numbers to 5	☐
13	Missing numbers to 10	☐
14	Counting to 10, addition to 10	☐
15	Subtraction from 10	☐

COPYMASTERS

101	Traffic cards – cut and paste	☐
105	Number snake addition	☐
106	Blank number snakes	☐
109	Addition stepping stones	☐
110	Blank addition stepping stones	☐
111	Addition	☐
112	Missing numbers	☐
113	Missing numbers	☐
114	Missing numbers	☐
115	Missing numbers	☐
116	Counting and addition	☐
117	Subtraction	☐

TOPIC WORKBOOK 4 PAGES

2	Identifying 3D shapes	☐
3	Identifying 3D shapes	☐
4	Language of measurement	☐
5	Language of measurement	☐
6	Language of position	☐
7	Language of measurement	☐
8	Continuing patterns	☐
9	Continuing patterns	☐
10	Language of position	☐
11	Language of position	☐
12	Numbers of sides of 2D shapes	☐
13	Drawing 2D shapes	☐
14	Reading analogue time	☐
15	Showing analogue time	☐

COPYMASTERS

102	Language of measurement	☐
103	Language of position, language of measurement	☐
104	Language of position, language of measurement	☐
107	Finishing patterns	☐
108	Pattern cards – cut and paste	☐
118	Numbers of sides of 2D shapes	☐
119	Drawing 2D shapes	☐
91	Analogue time	☐
92	Analogue time	☐
120	Analogue time (half-past)	☐
121	Analogue times (half-past)	☐

L1:1 Late!

Rupa and Lisa

SKILLS, CONCEPTS AND KNOWLEDGE

▶ Counting to 5

PRE-ASSESSMENT

Can the child:

▶ count up to 5 accurately?
▶ count randomly arranged sets of items?

The story

Pages 2 and 3 of the textbook introduce the characters Rupa and Lisa. Rupa is a tidy and organised person. She likes to collect materials for school, such as pencils, felt-pens and rubbers. Lisa, on the other hand, is more interested in her appearance, and likes to decorate her things with stickers, and badges showing her favourite stars.

Rupa and Lisa are firm friends, complementing each other's weaknesses with their individual strengths. Lisa shows a brash confidence to try anything, whilst Rupa balances this with a more reserved and thoughtful approach. Together they solve problems.

On these two pages they are getting ready to leave for school. The pages provide opportunities to discuss what children bring to school themselves, what time they get up and get ready, and what they are interested in.

Copymaster 1 provides a format for children to record their answers to questions in the textbook.

Maths content and resources

Children are asked to count and record the number of items belonging to each character. Picture clues are provided to help them identify the items to be counted.

Pages 2 to 5 of Number Workbook 1 offer more counting practice based on Rupa's and Lisa's homes. Illustrations of board games, cassette tapes, compact discs and posters from magazines relate to children's own interests. Children can be encouraged to discuss their own collections and interests, and to look at numbers arising from everyday examples brought from home. These workbook pages also ask children to read number words and write numerals to 10.

Copymasters 5 and 6 provide two more pages of counting 'homework', as in Number Workbook 1.

More counting activities

Stock taking in the classroom provides many opportunities for children to count for a purpose. As part of a check of the numbers of felt-pens, rubbers and pencil sharpeners in the classroom, children may be asked to write the number they have counted on a slip of paper or a label. These can be placed with the items to provide the basis for future counting; see if the same number is still there later in the day. This leads into using 'fewer than', 'more than', and 'difference', in practical contexts. Addition and subtraction may be introduced by asking questions like 'How many more do we need to make 5?' or 'We had 4 rubbers last time; how many are missing?'

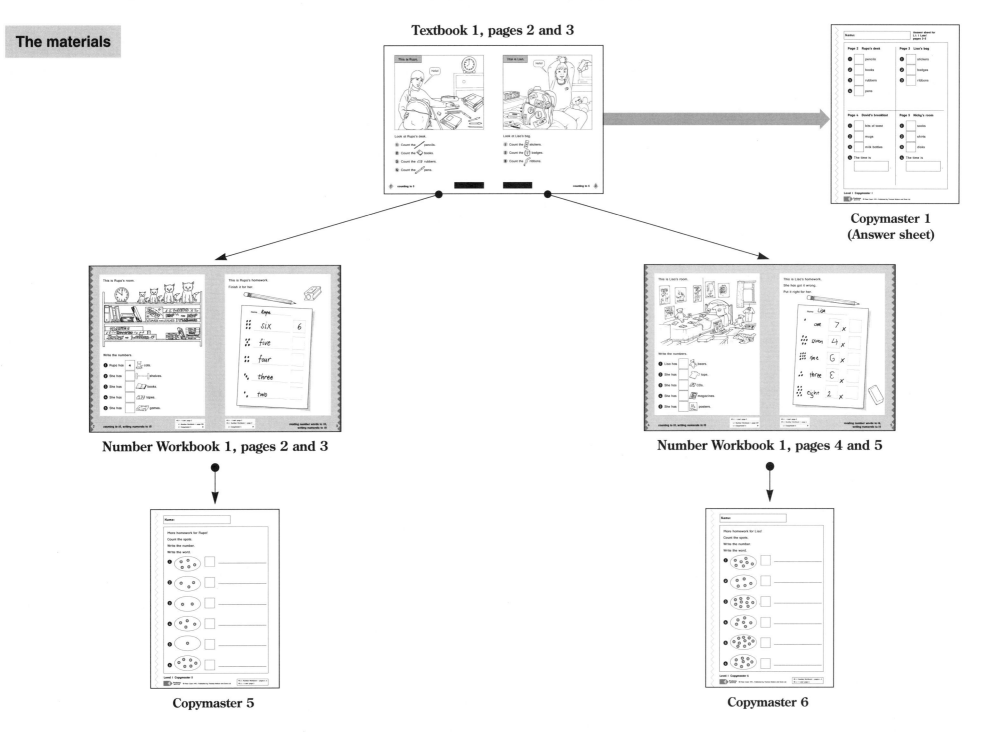

The materials

Textbook 1, pages 2 and 3

Copymaster 1
(Answer sheet)

Number Workbook 1, pages 2 and 3

Number Workbook 1, pages 4 and 5

Copymaster 5

Copymaster 6

David and Nicky

SKILLS, CONCEPTS AND KNOWLEDGE

▶ Counting to 5
▶ Reading analogue time
▶ Reading digital time

PRE-ASSESSMENT

Can the child:

▶ count up to 5 accurately?
▶ count randomly arranged sets of items?
▶ tell the time?

The story

David and Nicky are introduced on pages 4 and 5. Like Rupa and Lisa, they are firm friends. David is very keen on a variety of sports, whilst Nicky enjoys electronic games and anything to do with computers. They can both be over-enthusiastic, rushing into situations without thinking, but David is the more level-headed. David's school bag is enormous, and contains a treasure trove of all the things he needs, from food to footballs.

On these two pages the boys are just about to leave for school. The pages can be used as a starting point for discussions with children about what they have for breakfast, what they bring to school, and whether they play games on, or use, computers.

Copymaster 1 provides a format for children to record their answers to questions in the textbook.

Maths content and resources

These pages provide further counting experiences. Picture clues are provided, to help children identify the items to be counted. Children are asked to read and record analogue and digital times.

The counting activities on pages 6 to 9 of Number Workbook 1 are based on David's interest in sport and Nicky's computer. These contexts can be used to encourage children to look at what they like to do away from school. They can bring in posters or magazines about their hobbies, and look for numbers within them. 'More' and 'fewer' are introduced.

Copymasters 7 and 10 are worksheets using David's and Nicky's homes as a context. They provide children with more work on counting up to 10.

Analogue time is covered on pages 2 and 3 of Topic Workbook 1. Copymaster 11 is another analogue clock worksheet on time, and Copymaster 12 has blank clock faces, for teachers to prepare more if they are needed.

Pages 4 and 5 of Topic Workbook 1 and Copymaster 8 give work on reading and recording digital time. Further worksheets can be prepared from Copymaster 9.

Digital time

Digital timepieces are now common in the home. They allow children to communicate the time to others ('seven forty-five'), even though they may not be able to decode analogue clocks, or describe and calculate the passage of time. Time plays a part in the story in Textbook 1, as the characters become later and later for school. Copymaster 9 can be used for children to record significant times during the day, including time spent at home.

Analogue time

Telling the time using analogue clock faces can be difficult for children of any age. At this level it is sensible to revisit this regularly.

Copymaster 12 can also be used as a record sheet for children to record significant times during the day, including times spent at home.

A single clock face can be enlarged on the photocopier. Children can make moving hands by using paper fasteners to fix strips of card to the centre of the clock face. This will allow them to set the hands before recording their answers on paper.

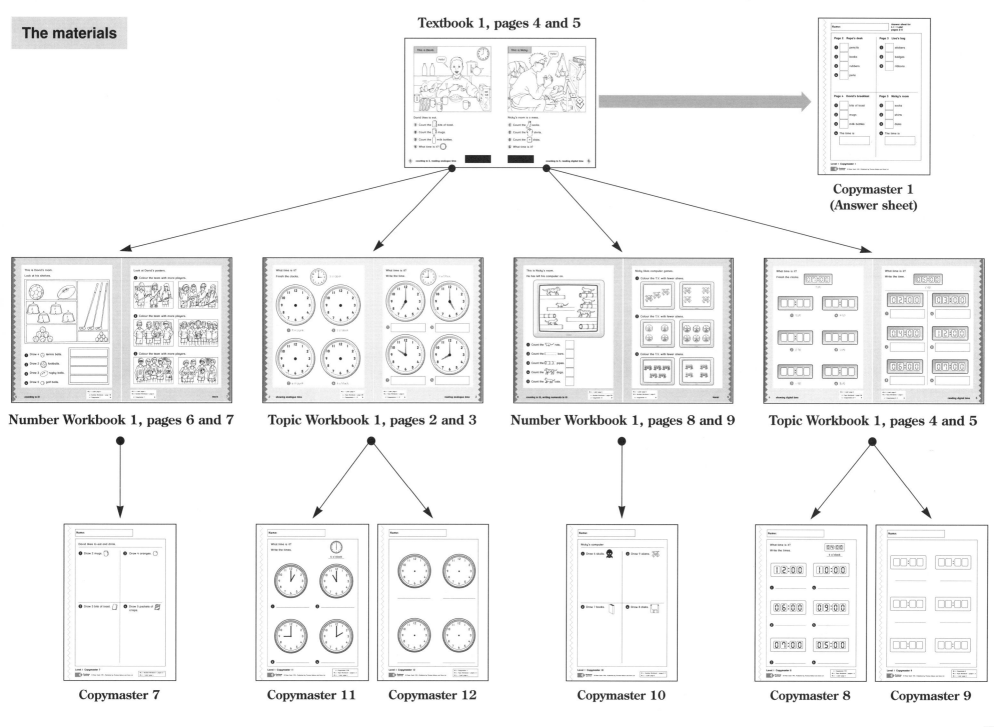

Textbook 1, pages 4 and 5

Copymaster 1
(Answer sheet)

Number Workbook 1, pages 6 and 7

Topic Workbook 1, pages 2 and 3

Number Workbook 1, pages 8 and 9

Topic Workbook 1, pages 4 and 5

Copymaster 7

Copymaster 11

Copymaster 12

Copymaster 10

Copymaster 8

Copymaster 9

The children meet up

SKILLS, CONCEPTS AND KNOWLEDGE

▶ Numerals to 10
▶ Identifying 2D shapes

PRE-ASSESSMENT

Can the child:

▶ recognise and order numbers up to 10?
▶ identify squares, triangles and circles?

The story

The scene on page 6 shows the children meeting outside their homes before they set off to school. They live in Carroll Close, which is a small square consisting of ten houses. Page 7 finds them already distracted by the swings in Polygon Park. Nicky and Lisa are happy to play, but David and Rupa are worried about being late. The pages can be used as a starting point for discussions about who children come to school with, and what they see and do on the way.

Copymaster 2 provides a format for children to record their answers to questions in the textbook.

Maths content and resources

Page 6 of the textbook offers an opportunity to look at children's own addresses, particularly house numbers. This should highlight the differences between Carroll Close and most other roads. For instance, houses are normally numbered alternately, with odd numbers on one side, and even numbers on the other.

Number ordering activities on pages 10 and 11 of Number Workbook 1 use real examples of how numbers are arranged on rulers, calculators and other keypads. All these can be investigated in real life.

Copymaster 14 provides numeral cards up to 10, for ordering activities and games.

Page 7 of the textbook may be used to introduce simple 2D shapes within everyday structures. The children may be encouraged to look at the 2D shapes around them, particularly those which are part of PE apparatus and playground furniture.

Pages 6 and 7 of Topic Workbook 1 introduce the rectangle and also ask children to name squares, triangles and circles. Copymaster 16 gives them the opportunity to draw simple 2D shapes, using spotty paper as a guide. It is important to emphasise that squares have equal sides. Using spotty paper will give them the chance to draw irregular as well as regular triangles.

Copymaster 15 can be made into cards for children to use in activities and games where they are asked to match shapes.

A simple counting and card matching game

You will need the cards on Copymaster 14. The cards are spread out, face down. The first child turns over two cards. If the numbers on the cards match, they keep the pair. If the cards do not match, they are put back, face up. The next player turns over one card. If it matches any cards which are face up, they keep the pair. If they do not find a match, they may turn over another card to try to find a pair. Whether they have been successful or not, play moves to the next person. The reason for leaving cards face up is to allow the children to concentrate on counting and matching, rather than memory. The winner is the child with the most cards at the end. The number range of the cards can be increased as children become more confident.

Ordering 1 to 10

For this game you will need the cards on Copymaster 14.

Two children can play. The cards are spread out, face down. Each child takes a card and turns it face up. They continue to take turns to choose a card. If the number on the card is sequential to the card they have, they can keep it. If not, it is returned, face down, to the middle. For example, if a child starts with 7 they can keep 6 or 8 but no other card; if a child has 6 and 7 they can keep 5 or 8. The winner is the first child to collect all the numbers from 1 to 10.

A family of shapes

For this game you will need the cards on Copymaster 15.

Four children can play. The cards are spread out, face down. Each child takes a turn to choose one card. The first shape they take is the shape they must collect. If a child picks a card with a circle, and someone is already collecting circles, they must put it back. The first child to collect all the cards for a particular shape is the winner.

Making a street

For this, you will need Copymaster 13.

Before the five house templates are cut out, it is a good idea to fold the sheet along all the vertical dotted lines. When each house has been cut out and folded, the two flaps for the base can be stuck together.

Children can use two sets of houses to make a model of Carroll Close. A plan of Carroll Close is to be found on Copymaster 17. Children can number all the doors from 1 to 10 and identify where the characters live.

This activity could be made more open-ended by allowing the children to arrange their houses to plan a small estate of their own design. Another way to extend the activity would be to use the original templates as the basis for making new templates for larger buildings.

The materials

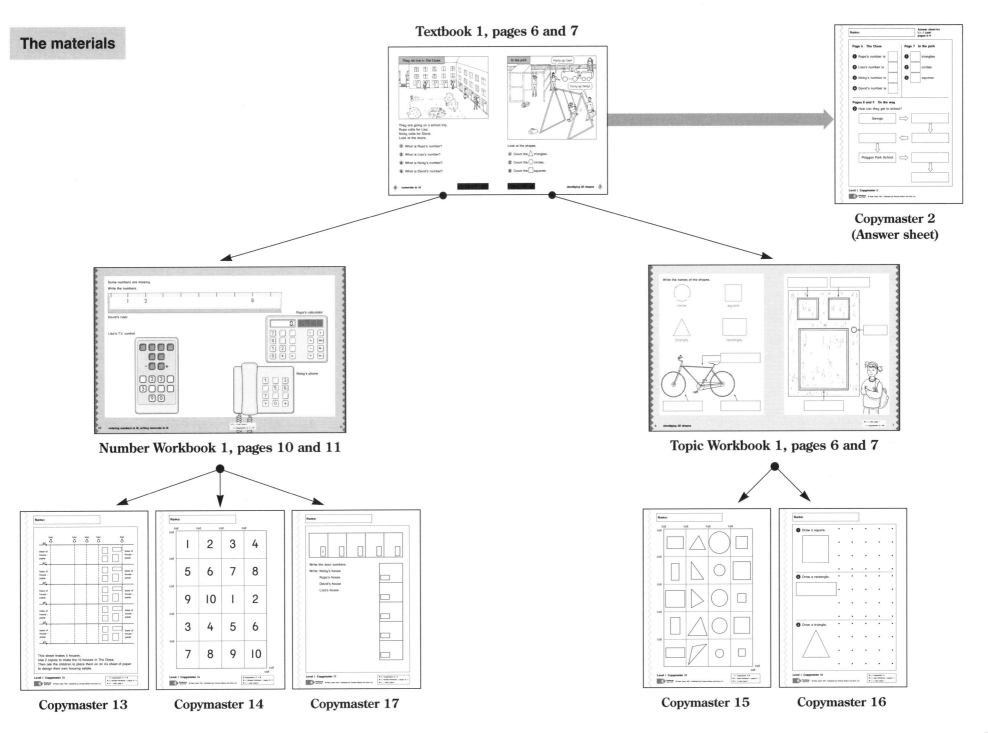

Textbook 1, pages 6 and 7

Copymaster 2
(Answer sheet)

Number Workbook 1, pages 10 and 11

Topic Workbook 1, pages 6 and 7

Copymaster 13

Copymaster 14

Copymaster 17

Copymaster 15

Copymaster 16

Getting to school on time

SKILLS, CONCEPTS AND KNOWLEDGE

▶ Planning routes

PRE-ASSESSMENT

Can the child:

▶ plan a simple route?

The story

The children are still in the park, and now find themselves late for school. They need to find the quickest way to get there. The tunnel is the obvious short-cut.

The pages can be used as a starting point for discussions with children about how they plan their own routes to school. Do they call for a friend? Do they stop and play? Do they need to visit the shop to buy something for their lunch?

Copymaster 2 provides a format for children to record their suggested routes for Lisa and her friends to get to school quickly. It is not necessary to use all the boxes provided. For children who have difficulties with writing, the map on Copymaster 18 provides the opportunity to draw the route (or routes). It may also be used to encourage children to draw their own maps.

Maths content and resources

The textbook pages show the problem and provide a map of the area, so that children can try to visualise alternative routes.

Activities on pages 8 and 9 of Topic Workbook 1 are based on a trip to the shops and a visit to the park. Children show, by drawing, the routes that Nicky and Rupa take. These contexts can be used to encourage children to discuss what they would do in a similar situation. Also, they can talk about whether they go to the shops, and how their local park is set out.

Copymasters 19 and 20 provide simple mazes, which can be modified by teachers to extend their usefulness. Once a photocopy has been made, correction fluid can be used to open new pathways, and black felt-pen to close certain routes. There are many comics and puzzle books which include mazes, and these can be easily incorporated.

Children will most easily relate to plans of areas with which they are familiar. The most common plans made in schools are of the classroom, the school itself, and children's routes to school. It is important that children understand the purpose of such plans, so they feel that they are doing the work for a reason. It is also important to allow children to devise their own conventions and scales.

Making a plan of the classroom

A good way to introduce this activity is to ask children to discuss ways of arranging the classroom. Are things stored in the best places? Is there enough room to move about? Are the tables too big, or too small, for the numbers of people sitting at them, and for the things they need to do? The aim should be to prepare a plan of the existing layout and then try to make alternative arrangements.

Templates of tables can be provided, or the children can devise some of their own (circular or rectangular tables would support other work at this level). The templates can then be moved around on a sheet of paper. The templates and paper should be roughly to the same scale as the original plan of the classroom. Children may find A4 paper restricting to work with and, if possible, they should have access to larger sheets.

Making a plan of the school

This is a more difficult exercise, and should involve the children in moving around the school as they develop and modify their plans. Once again, giving the children a reason for the work is important. Are there enough fire exits? Is the school easy to get into for welcome visitors? Is it too accessible for unwelcome visitors? Are children of the same age near to each other? Is the library easy to get to for all classes? Again, templates may be useful and children should have the opportunity to work on large sheets of paper which can be extended as they add new information.

How do I get to school?

Children can be encouraged to draw their route, or routes, to school. This need not be in traditional map format. A simple line with pictures or words to describe landmarks is enough. This is a good opportunity to use the words 'left' and 'right', and for children to devise their own symbols and codes for describing places and movements. Their plans can be compared to a simple local map.

The materials

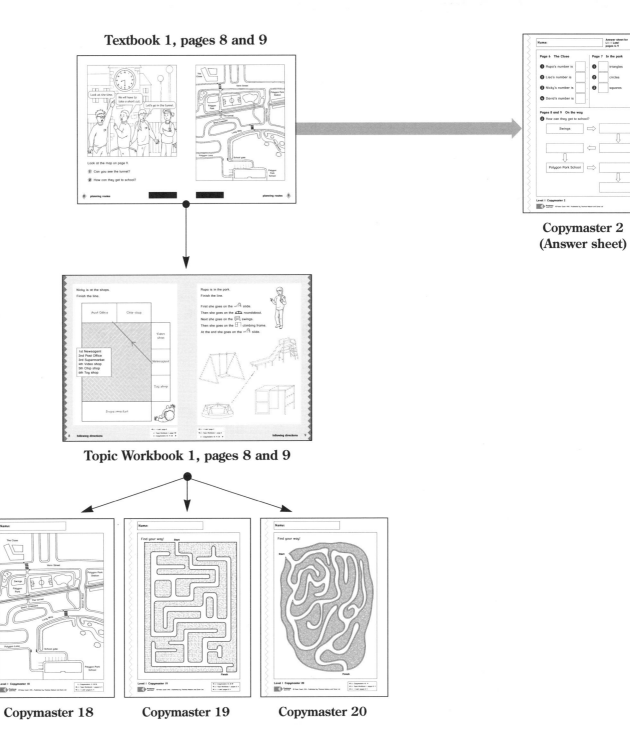

Textbook 1, pages 8 and 9

Copymaster 2
(Answer sheet)

Topic Workbook 1, pages 8 and 9

Copymaster 18   Copymaster 19   Copymaster 20

The tunnel

SKILLS, CONCEPTS AND KNOWLEDGE

▶ Language of position
▶ Continuing patterns

PRE-ASSESSMENT

Can the child:

▶ use 'left' and 'right'?
▶ use 'inside' and 'outside'?
▶ copy a pattern?
▶ continue a pattern?

The story

The characters have decided to use the tunnel, as it is the only way to get to school on time. In front of the tunnel, they still have the options of going left or right to avoid using it. The tunnel is being redecorated. Inside the tunnel, they find a tile pattern and try to complete it. This is yet another distraction to make them even later for school, and Rupa points this out.

Copymaster 3 provides a format for children to record their answers to questions in the textbook, and to copy and complete the tile pattern. They will need 1- or 2-centimetre squared paper to devise their own patterns.

Maths content and resources

The textbook pages cover two elements. Page 10 is largely concerned with the language of position. As with so much work at this level, it is most valuable to link the language to practical activities. Similarly, the pattern work on page 11 is ideally introduced, or supported, by using real tile patterns as models.

Page 10 of Topic Workbook 1 provides extra practice in identifying 'inside' and 'outside'. Page 11 covers 'over', 'under', 'left' and 'right'.

Pages 12 and 13 in Topic Workbook 1 extend the pattern-making activities, using flowers and squares. Children can be encouraged to invent their own patterns.

Copymaster 22 is a worksheet with more patterns to complete. These are based on diagonally, horizontally and vertically divided squares. Copymaster 21 provides cards which can be used to support this work practically.

Activities using the language of position

It is difficult in a busy classroom to make a point of using specific words. However, certain activities do lend themselves to this. PE sessions where apparatus is being used allow teachers to use many position words. Some examples are:

'Go *up* one step.'

'Come *down* very slowly.'

'Groups, move to the next activity on your *left*.'

'Slide *under* the apparatus.'

It is difficult to be aware of every opportunity for using position words during a concentrated session planned for physical activity. However, it is worthwhile even if only a couple of words such as 'up' and 'down' are used.

Logo, Turtle and other programmable machines

'Left' and 'right' become so much more important when children are using independent programmable machines. They will try, and try again, to make the robots go where they want them to. Even with a very limited amount of classroom apparatus, it is easy to build bridges and tunnels so that they have to go under and over certain obstacles. They can even be set obstacle courses of objects to knock over, such as cylinders and boxes. Time, practice and a reliable robot are all essential if children are to use the activity to refine their use of instructions, and also of position words.

Following the pattern

For this game you will need Copymaster 21.

One set of pattern cards can be used, initially. The cards are shared out equally between two players. One of them starts by placing two cards together on the table. The next player places two more cards beside the first two to repeat the pattern.

They continue to take turns to place pairs of cards until all the cards are gone. Initially, children will tend to place cards in a line. After playing a few times, they can be encouraged to spread out in other directions.

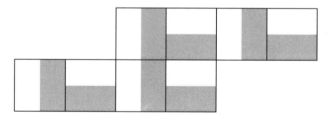

Whenever possible, it is useful to ask the children to explain how the pattern is designed and to encourage them to discuss and check each other's work.

The game can be extended by using three or four cards at a time. This will probably require two or more sets of cards.

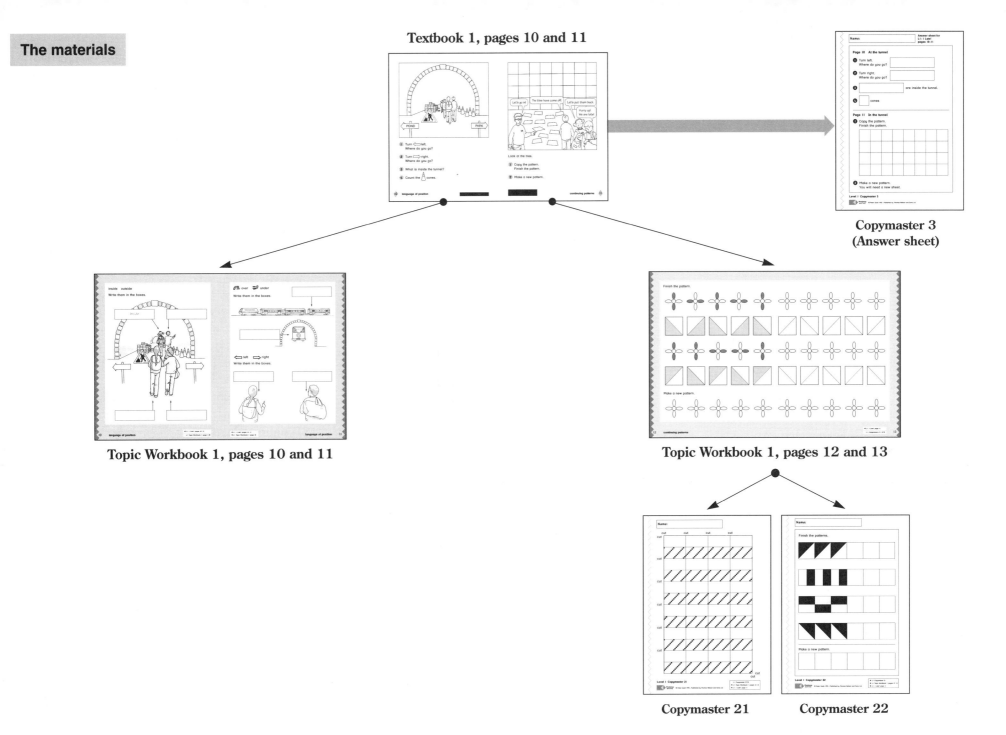

Textbook 1, pages 10 and 11

Copymaster 3
(Answer sheet)

Topic Workbook 1, pages 10 and 11

Topic Workbook 1, pages 12 and 13

Copymaster 21

Copymaster 22

The other end of the tunnel

SKILLS, CONCEPTS AND KNOWLEDGE

▶ Identifying 3D shapes
▶ Language of position
▶ Ordering numbers to 10

PRE-ASSESSMENT

Can the child:
▶ name cuboids and cylinders?
▶ order numbers to 10?

The story

Having reached the other end of the tunnel, the characters find still more distractions. They stop to watch a train passing over the tunnel, and then find hopscotch markings on the pavement. The train on page 12 can be used to help match the names of simple 3D shapes to everyday objects, and identify 'front' and 'back'. The hopscotch game on page 13 is a number ordering activity.

Copymaster 4 provides a format for children to record their answers to questions in the textbook. The hopscotch markings may be used to create more number ordering activities.

Maths content and resources

Page 12 shows cylinders and cuboids in an everyday context. Cylinders are used for the bulk transport and storage of liquids. Solid objects tend to be stored in box-shaped containers, which are easier to stack. Pages 10 and 11 of Topic Workbook 1 develop the work on the language of position which is also featured on page 12 of the textbook.

The hopscotch game on page 13 shows one form of playground marking. Other games which may be found in school also use number ordering skills, for example, snakes and ladders.

Pages 14 and 15 in Topic Workbook 1 involve naming pictures of everyday 3D objects. Ideally, children will have access to real 3D shapes to handle, match and sort before doing this work. Some criteria for sorting 3D shapes are:

Which shapes roll well?
Which shapes do not?
Which shapes are easy to stack?
Can some shapes be stacked in one way but not in another?

3D shape cards, which can be made from Copymaster 23, can be used for matching games, or as labels when sorting real 3D objects. Copymaster 24 is another worksheet asking children to name basic 3D shapes in everyday objects.

The number ordering activities on pages 12 and 13 of Number Workbook 1 are based on playground games. The pages provide opportunities to discuss how, or even if, children would use these. The children can be encouraged to make suggestions as to games which could be played, using the number square up to 9, or the number snake.

Copymaster 25 provides a set of number spot cards with different numbers of spots, up to 10, on each. Copymaster 26 is an additional number ordering worksheet.

A simple counting card game

For this game you will need the cards on Copymaster 25 (with 1 to 5 spots).

The cards are shuffled and the first one is turned over, in front of the group. The first child to count and announce the correct number of spots wins the card. The overall winner is the child with the most cards at the end, and they become the dealer next time.

Children can quickly learn to play this independently, and can check each other. The number range of the cards can be increased as the children become more confident and skilled. The game also helps to develop estimation skills. Observing children whilst they are playing the game will give clues as to those who are counting with their fingers, those who are scanning with their eyes, and those who are estimating. Normal playing cards may be used to introduce the numerals alongside the spots.

Number ordering bingo

For this game you will need two sets of the cards on Copymaster 25. Two bingo cards can be made from the same copymaster.

Children take turns to turn over the cards. If they have a space for the card they have chosen, they can place it on their bingo card. If the space is already occupied, the card must be returned, face down. The winner is the first player to complete their bingo card.

The game can be made more difficult if children have to find 1 spot first, 2 spots second and so on.

3D shape bingo

For this game you will need Copymaster 23.

The game is played in exactly the same way as the one above, with children having to match the shape pictures on a set of cards to the bingo cards in front of them. When preparing the bingo cards, it is a good idea to split Copymaster 23 vertically down the centre line, to make two cards with ten shapes on each.

The materials

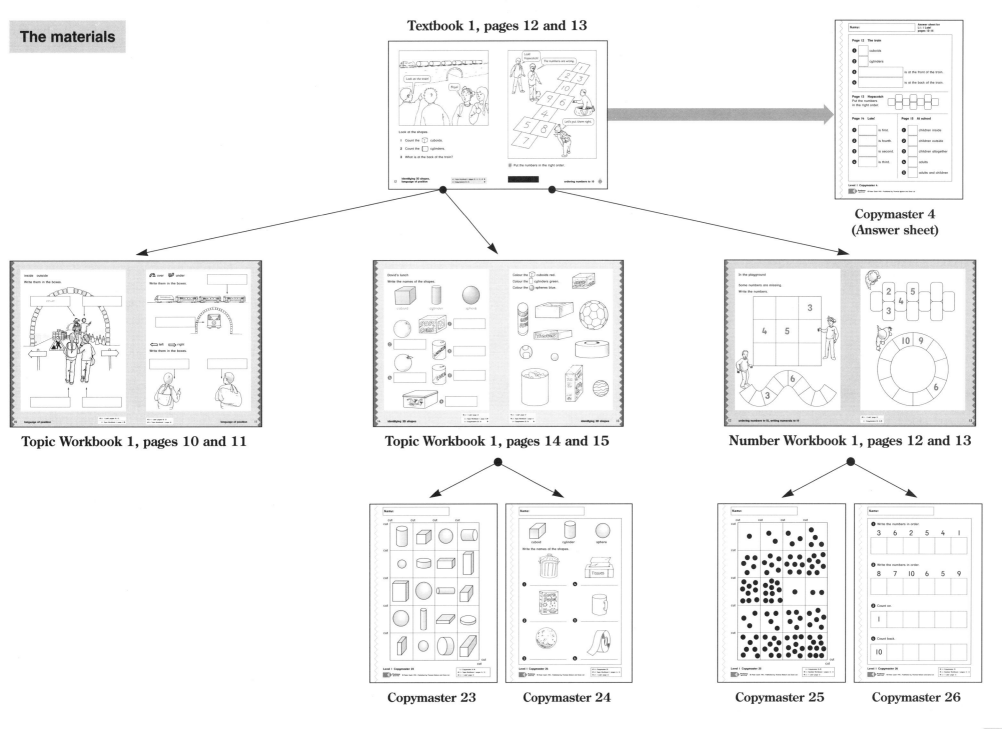

Textbook 1, pages 12 and 13

Copymaster 4 (Answer sheet)

Topic Workbook 1, pages 10 and 11

Topic Workbook 1, pages 14 and 15

Number Workbook 1, pages 12 and 13

Copymaster 23

Copymaster 24

Copymaster 25

Copymaster 26

The dash to school

SKILLS, CONCEPTS AND KNOWLEDGE

▶ Language of position
▶ Addition to 10

PRE-ASSESSMENT

Can the child:

▶ describe a sequence using 'first' to 'fourth'?
▶ combine two numbers by counting?
▶ take one number from another?

The story

Rupa, Lisa, Nicky and David make a final 'mad dash' to get to school on time. When they arrive, they see their teacher waiting by the bus. Some children are already on the bus. It is apparent that they are going on a school trip.

The pages can be used as a basis for talking about how we describe the order of things, using 'first', 'second', 'third', 'fourth' and so on. These words can be related to motor races or athletics, which are presented extensively on television. The pages also provide the opportunity for children to suggest where the class might be going on their trip.

Copymaster 4 provides a format for children to record their answers to questions in the textbook.

Maths content and resources

Page 14 of the textbook is a simple introduction to the ordinal words 'first' to 'fourth'. Language occurs naturally in many classroom situations, for example 'First, get some paper.'

Activities on pages 14 and 15 of Number Workbook 1 reflect the work on page 15 of the textbook. This is the first visit to addition in the story, and children may rely heavily on counting. They are likely to need time and some help with the work. The workbook pages are based on a bus journey. It is a good idea to provide some physical representation of the passengers such as small cubes, so that children can put them on and take them off the pictures of the buses.

Copymasters 27 to 32 are further worksheets which use pictures to show addition situations, covering all the number facts to 10.

At this stage it is not expected that the children will memorise number facts like $2 + 3 = 5$. The emphasis should be on using practical materials and identifying everyday situations in which addition and subtraction appear. It is also important to emphasise that addition makes numbers bigger, and subtraction makes them smaller.

First to 10

For this game, the following can be used: counters, bottle tops or bricks such as Unifix or Multilink, and a die with numbers 0 to 3 on its faces. (If a die is not available, one can be made by marking a wooden cube with spots or numerals.) Two or more children can play and they will need at least 10 counters per child. The counters are placed in the middle.

Children take turns to throw the die and collect the number of counters indicated by the numbers or spots. It is very important to add rules to encourage children to explain to each other what they are doing. For example, after a throw, they could be asked to say something like:

'I have 3 bricks. I need 7 more. That will be 1, 2, 3, 4, 5, 6, 7, 8, 9, 10.'

Introducing new language over a period of time will help children to associate mathematical words such as 'and', 'add', 'plus', 'makes' and 'equals' with the operation of addition. Also, they can be encouraged to discuss and check each other's answers.

After a while, children will begin to predict what may happen next:

'She only needs 2 more.'
'I want a 3.'

When there is time, observing children's counting strategies will help to assess their skill levels. For example, if they have 5 and throw 3, initially children are likely to count from 1: '1, 2, 3, 4, 5, 6, 7, 8.' A breakthrough occurs when they begin to count on from the number they have already: '5, 6, 7, 8.'

They may transfer the counting to their fingers, or look into the distance as they count in their heads. Finally, they may begin to remember certain combinations, particularly $1 + 1$, $2 + 2$ and so on.

To incorporate subtraction into the game, children can start with 10 and remove the value of the throw each time. It is particularly useful to use interlocking cubes made into rods of 10. The cubes can then be broken off as they are subtracted. Initially, children will break them off one at a time. Eventually they will count the number to be subtracted and break them all off together. Learning, and becoming used to playing, games like these is time well spent. Once children know the routine, the number ranges can be extended all the way up to three-digit numbers.

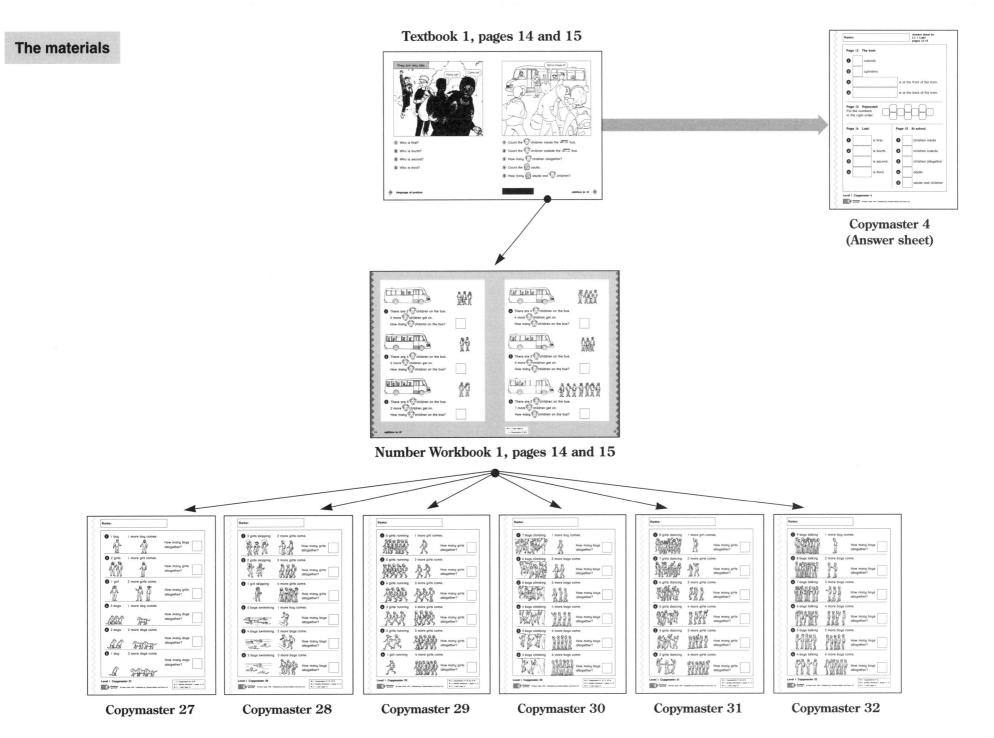

Textbook 1, pages 14 and 15

Copymaster 4
(Answer sheet)

Number Workbook 1, pages 14 and 15

Copymaster 27   Copymaster 28   Copymaster 29   Copymaster 30   Copymaster 31   Copymaster 32

L1:2 On the bus

Getting on the bus

SKILLS, CONCEPTS AND KNOWLEDGE

▶ Counting to 10

PRE-ASSESSMENT

Can the child:

▶ count up to 10 accurately?

The story

The children are boarding the bus and settling down to begin the journey. The teacher tells them that they are going to visit Polygon Castle, and that they will stop for lunch at twelve o'clock. There is a pictorial reminder of who the characters are.

The pages provide a context for discussing school trips which children have been on, or which are being planned.

Copymaster 33 provides a format for children to record their answers to questions in the textbook.

Maths content and resources

The textbook pages revisit counting up to 10. This is to give children who are unsure another chance to practise. For children who are counting well, the pages offer an opportunity to use their skills and gain confidence from their success.

Pages 2 to 5 of Number Workbook 2 are more pages of counting. Sometimes items are mixed up so that children will need to sort and count carefully. It is a good idea to encourage them to check their counting before writing their answers.

Copymasters 37 to 40 are worksheets, providing further practice with counting. Copymaster 38 also covers 'the same'. On Copymaster 40, children have to draw coats and bags on pegs, and count how many pegs are left. This is a subtraction exercise.

Guess how many

For this game, the following can be used: interlocking cubes, such as Unifix or Multilink, and a box, book or cloth, to hide them.

The children play this in pairs. One child looks away while the other takes a handful of cubes (this is unlikely to be more than 10). The cubes are counted by the child who took them, and then hidden under the cloth, in the box, or behind the book. The other child then has to guess how many were taken, by suggesting a number. The child who hid the cubes responds by saying:

'No, more!' or,
'No, less!' or,
'Right!'

The cubes are then revealed and counted again by both children, to check. The players then reverse roles and repeat the game.

An extra counting activity can be introduced into the game if children keep a tally of the number of guesses they needed before they got the right answer. This can be done by making marks on paper, or by dropping a counter into a pot for each guess made.

The materials

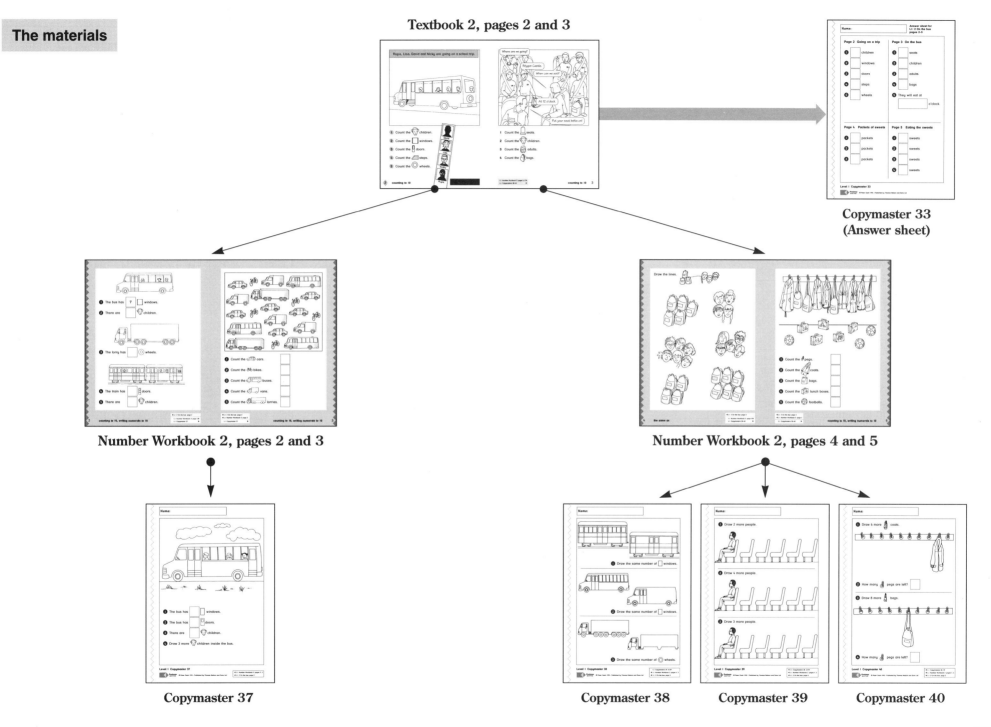

Textbook 2, pages 2 and 3

Copymaster 33
(Answer sheet)

Number Workbook 2, pages 2 and 3

Number Workbook 2, pages 4 and 5

Copymaster 37

Copymaster 38

Copymaster 39

Copymaster 40

Time for some sweets

SKILLS, CONCEPTS AND KNOWLEDGE

▶ Addition to 10
▶ Subtraction from 10

PRE-ASSESSMENT

Can the child:

▶ recognise when to add?
▶ add by counting?
▶ recognise when to subtract?
▶ subtract by deleting?

The story

On the journey, the children are talking about how many packets of sweets they have brought with them. David then offers some of his to the others. The pages can be used to talk about whether eating sweets on school trips is a good idea. As well as the dental issue, there are the problems of litter and general stickiness!

Copymaster 33 provides a format for children to record their answers to questions in the textbook.

Maths content and resources

On page 4 of the textbook, children have to identify the characters and add the number of packets of sweets they have. The totals are less than 10, until the final question where the total of all the packets is 10. Page 5 shows the children giving out sweets, in sets of 2, from their packets. This offers the chance to assess whether children can subtract by counting down 1 or 2 at a time.

Activities on pages 6 and 7 of Number Workbook 2 continue the work on addition, using the contexts of a bus journey and everyday objects. Pages 8 and 9 provide more simple subtraction situations.

Copymasters 41 and 42 are worksheets on addition which ask children to draw more objects as well as count up totals. Copymaster 43 is a worksheet on subtraction, where children can cross out sweets to show the number taken away, and then count those left.

On Copymaster 44, children have to colour the set with 'fewer' objects.

All sorts of dice-based games, such as ludo or snakes and ladders, provide valuable counting activities, both in counting the spots on the dice, and in moving counters along number tracks. Pairs of dice, numbered from 1 to 6 or 0 to 5, allow many number combinations to be generated in a very short time.

Target numbers

For this game, you will need two standard dice and five cubes, such as Multilink or Unifix.

Two or more children can play. The five cubes are the prizes, and are placed in the centre. The basic idea is that the number of cubes you start with is the target number for the dice throws. Children take turns to throw the dice, collecting cubes accordingly. When all five cubes have been claimed, the game is over, and the person with the most is the winner.

This game can be played many times with different numbers of cubes. Children may be encouraged to choose their own target numbers up to 10. The only numbers which will not work are 0 and 1.

Children can be encouraged to suggest alternative rules or other dice games they know.

The materials

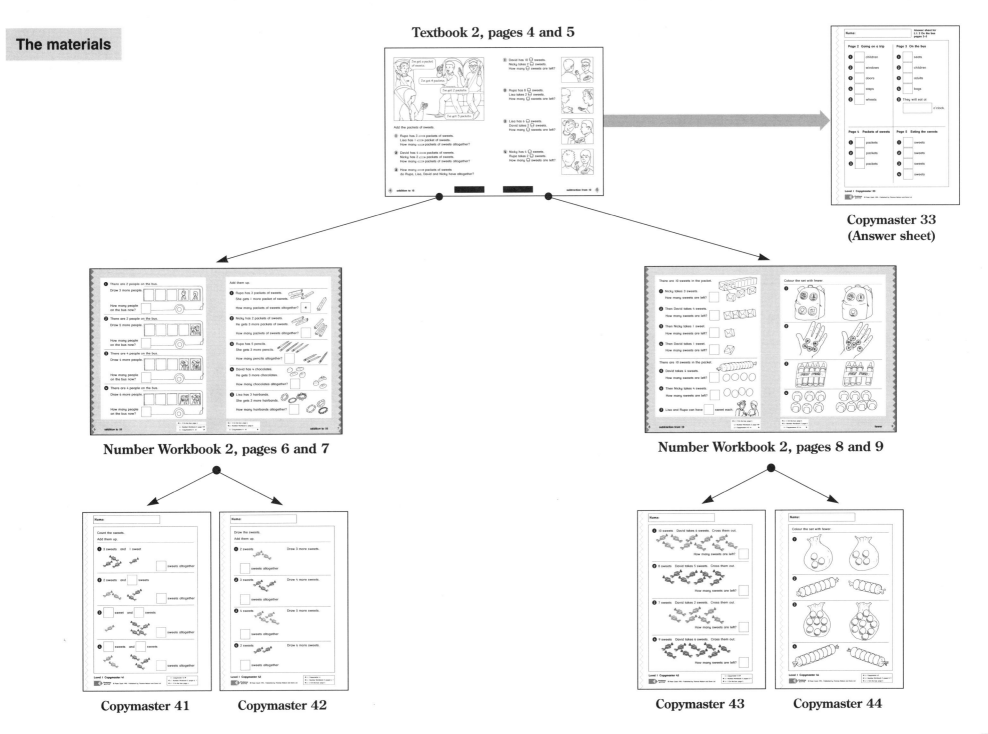

Textbook 2, pages 4 and 5

**Copymaster 33
(Answer sheet)**

Number Workbook 2, pages 6 and 7

Number Workbook 2, pages 8 and 9

Copymaster 41

Copymaster 42

Copymaster 43

Copymaster 44

Traffic signs

SKILLS, CONCEPTS AND KNOWLEDGE

▶ Identifying 2D shapes
▶ Language of direction

PRE-ASSESSMENT

Can the child:
▶ identify squares, rectangles, triangles and circles?
▶ identify left and right?

The story

The bus journey continues, and on the way the children see some traffic signs. Eventually they see one which shows that they are near the picnic area. The pages can be used to introduce the use of 2D shapes for traffic signs, for example:

Red triangles are warnings.
Red circles are orders not to do something.
Blue circles are orders to do something.
Blue or green rectangles give information or directions.

Copymaster 34 provides a format for children to record their answers to questions in the textbook.

Maths content and resources

The textbook pages introduce traffic signs and some of the symbols they carry.

Activities on pages 2 to 3 of Topic Workbook 2 are also based on traffic signs. Copymaster 45 provides a set of cards showing 2D shapes as traffic signs. These can be used for games, or, if enlarged on a photocopier, they can provide the basis for children to make their own signs. Copymaster 46 gives practice in drawing 2D shapes.

Pages 4 and 5 of Topic Workbook 2 are concerned with following directions and the language of position. Copymasters 47 and 48 are worksheets which provide further practice in using the language of direction.

These contexts can be used to survey signs in the local area. The pages can be used as a starting point for discussions about signs around the school: for instance, which ones give help, which instructions, which warnings? Children could try to devise their own signs for use in school.

At this level, there are many practical activities to reinforce the language of position. Programmable toys, such as Roamer, are ideal vehicles for children to negotiate obstacle courses. To link with work on traffic signs, a course could be set with arrows showing directions and 'No entry' or 'No right turn' signs. Copymaster 45 can be used for these. A simple road system can be made with chalk, or masking tape, depending on the floor surface. Children can negotiate it by giving commands.

Matching shapes

For this game you will need Copymaster 45.

Children can try to draw some road signs on the cards.

It is not necessary to use all the cards. Children can sort out just two sets of shapes, such as circles and triangles. The cards are spread out, face down, on the table. It can be helpful to arrange them in a regular pattern. This will help children to remember where certain cards are. Players take turns to turn over two cards at a time. If they are in the same family of shapes, they keep them. If not, they are returned to their original positions, face down. Play continues until all the cards are matched. The winner is the child with the most cards.

These kinds of game can be easily modified to use more, or fewer, cards, and children can include shape cards which they have made themselves.

The materials

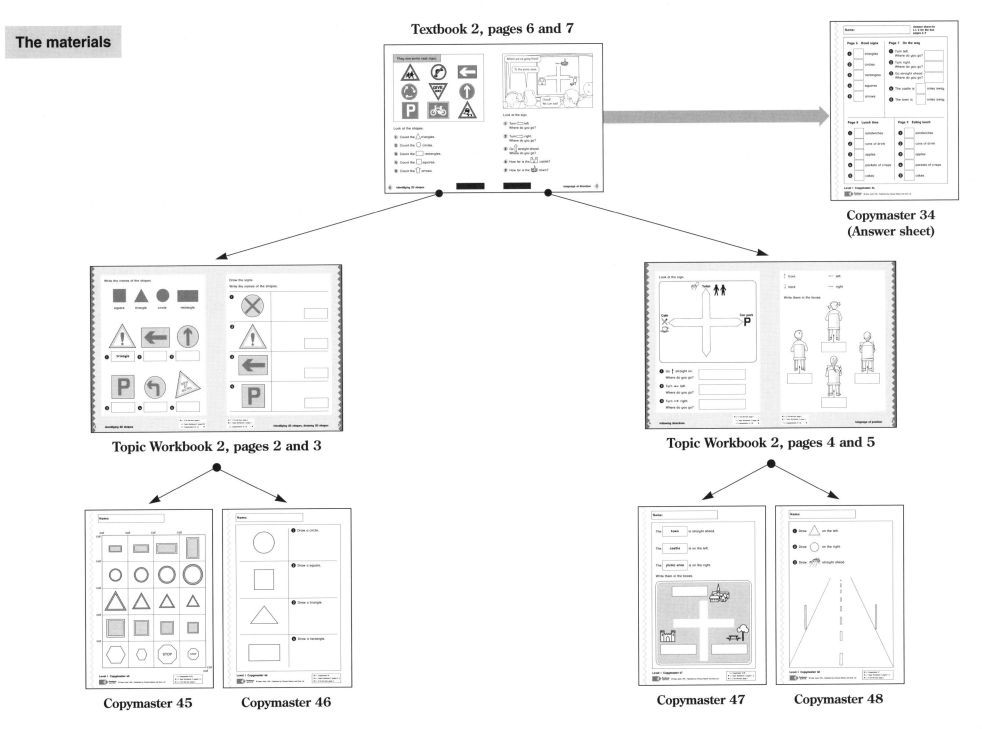

Textbook 2, pages 6 and 7

Copymaster 34
(Answer sheet)

Topic Workbook 2, pages 2 and 3

Topic Workbook 2, pages 4 and 5

Copymaster 45

Copymaster 46

Copymaster 47

Copymaster 48

At the picnic area

SKILLS, CONCEPTS AND KNOWLEDGE

▶ Addition to 10
▶ Subtraction from 10

PRE-ASSESSMENT

Can the child:

▶ recognise when to add?
▶ add by counting?
▶ recognise when to subtract?
▶ subtract by deleting?

The story

The characters have arrived at the picnic area and have unpacked their lunch boxes. They are comparing the contents. After eating, they see what is left over. The pages can be used as a starting point for talking about children's own preferences for packed lunches. Small surveys of favourite sandwich fillings, crisp flavours, fruits, drinks or biscuits can lead to some useful work on handling data, particularly if this is related to a real outing. Wrappers can be collected and sorted, and the shape and nature of packaging investigated.

Copymaster 34 provides a format for children to record their answers to questions in the textbook.

Maths content and resources

The textbook pages have strong visual clues to help children to add up lists of items in the packed lunches on page 8, and work out how much is left on page 9.

Activities on pages 10 and 11 Number Workbook 2 are based directly on the addition work in the textbook. Pages 12 and 13 provide work on subtraction.

Copymasters 49 and 50 are worksheets providing further practice in addition. Copymaster 51 is a subtraction worksheet, and Copymaster 52 provides a set of cards showing different numbers of cans and bottles for addition and subtraction games.

An addition game

For this game you will need two sets of the cards on Copymaster 52. Use only the cards showing 1, 2, 3, 4 or 5 items (either bottles or cans). This means that children will not encounter combinations which add up to more than 10.

The cards are spread out, face down, on the table. Players take turns to select two. They state the two numbers, and what they add up to. If everyone in the group agrees that the total is correct, the player can keep the cards. If the total is incorrect, the player has to replace them. The winner is the child with the most cards at the end.

These cards may also be used to investigate number combinations co-operatively. Children may be asked to look at a set of cards from 1 to 10, and find all the pairs they can which add up to a particular number, for example 7. They should find:

1 and 6
2 and 5
3 and 4

They may suggest 7 by itself, and they should have 8, 9 and 10 left over. Even numbers such as 6 will present problems in this game, because there is only one 3 in the set. However, the problem with these numbers can be overcome by using two sets of cards.

In this case children should also find the reverse of combinations. For instance, the reverse of 3 and 4 is 4 and 3.

A subtraction game

For this game you will need the cards on Copymaster 52 (bottles or cans from 1 to 10).

Before play begins the cards should be separated into two piles: from 1 to 5 and from 6 to 10.

At each turn, children take one card from each pile. They then subtract the smaller number from the larger number. To win the cards, they must state the subtraction and the answer. This may be a useful game for introducing the expression 'difference'.

These games can be played co-operatively as well as competitively, and children can be encouraged to suggest new versions or additional rules.

The materials

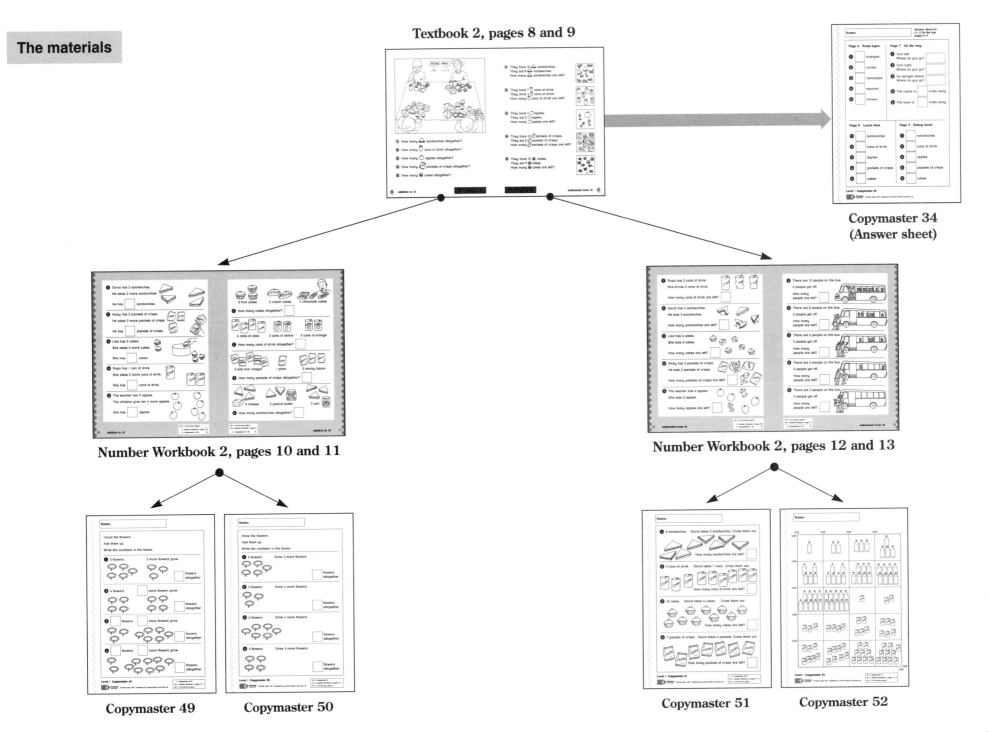

Textbook 2, pages 8 and 9

Copymaster 34
(Answer sheet)

Number Workbook 2, pages 10 and 11

Number Workbook 2, pages 12 and 13

Copymaster 49

Copymaster 50

Copymaster 51

Copymaster 52

After lunch

SKILLS, CONCEPTS AND KNOWLEDGE

▶ Identifying 3D shapes
▶ Addition to 10

PRE-ASSESSMENT

Can the child:

▶ identify cuboids, cylinders, spheres and cones?
▶ recognise when to add?
▶ add by counting?

The story

The characters have finished their lunch and are about to clear up. The picnic table shows everyday examples of common 3D shapes. The characters then clear away the litter before having a short playtime. Page 10 can be used to relate familiar objects to their 3D shape names. Page 11 uses the theme of litter to provide more work on addition to 10. This could be extended into looking at litter in school and surveying the types of thing people throw away.

Copymaster 35 provides a format for children to record their answers to questions in the textbook.

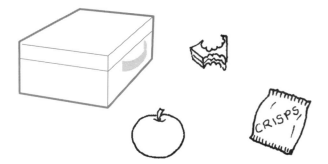

Maths content and resources

When children have identified the 3D shapes on the textbook page, it would be worthwhile to build a collection of everyday objects, such as cans and boxes, which have these shapes. These could be displayed alongside regular geometric shapes. The display can then be used as a resource for discussions about the features which the objects have in common such as the number of corners or curved surfaces.

Pages 6 and 7 of Topic Workbook 2 use similar examples to those in the textbook for identifying and drawing examples of 3D shapes.

Copymaster 53 asks children to map everyday objects to examples of regular 3D shapes. Copymaster 54 offers a chance for children to draw straight, curved, pointed and round shapes.

Activities on pages 14 and 15 of Number Workbook 2 revisit addition and subtraction. This work is continued on Copymasters 55 and 56, which are worksheets using the contexts of containers and litter.

Investigating boxes

Practical work with 3D shapes will involve rolling and building with them. Modern packaging also offers children the opportunity to dismantle and reconstruct the shapes.

Miniature cereal boxes are an ideal starting point. They are not too fiddly, and they are made of card which is relatively easy to cut, yet strong enough to sustain repeated handling. Before using them, children or teachers should use glue or tape to seal any flaps which have been opened.

The opposite faces of boxes can be coloured or marked. When the box is dismantled, these can be matched up by laying one on top of the other to compare areas, lengths and widths.

Boxes can be cut carefully along their edges to separate all six faces. After looking at areas and opposite faces, turn them over so that the plain card is uppermost. Children can decorate these with designs of their own. The challenge then is to put the box back together. This is done most easily with adhesive tape. Masking tape is quite good, because it allows errors to be corrected.

To develop the activities, children can be encouraged to modify the boxes with openings and cut-outs. Eventually, they may be able to start with their own rectangles of card and devise their own boxes. Card cylinders, Easter egg boxes and cosmetic packages can all be used in a similar way.

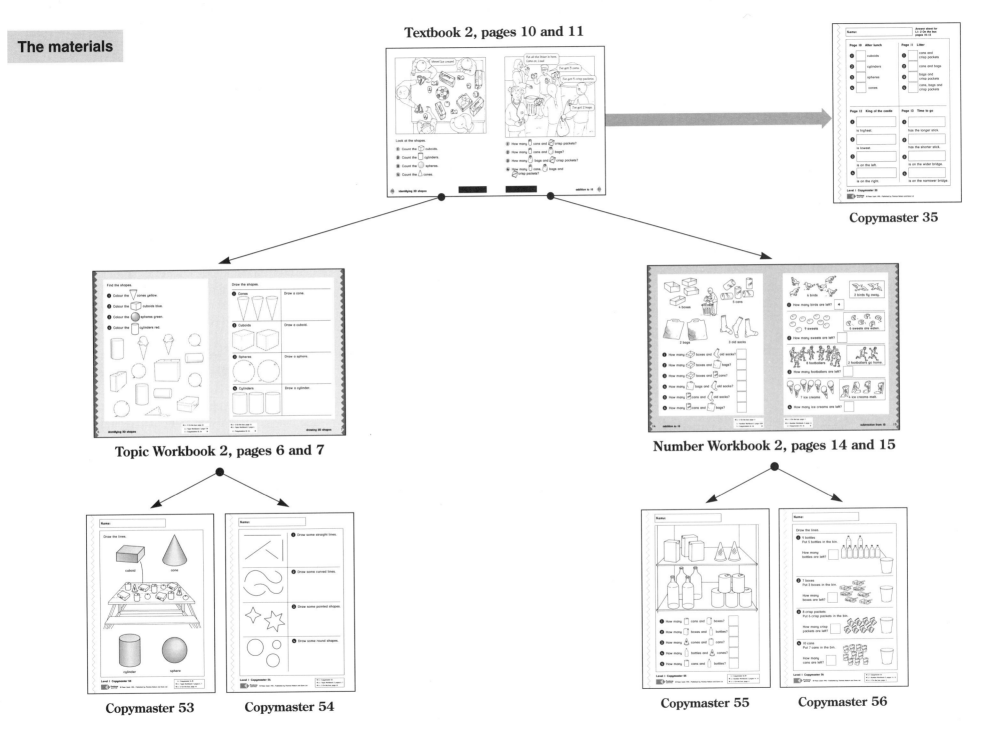

The materials

Textbook 2, pages 10 and 11

Copymaster 35

Topic Workbook 2, pages 6 and 7

Number Workbook 2, pages 14 and 15

Copymaster 53

Copymaster 54

Copymaster 55

Copymaster 56

Playtime

SKILLS, CONCEPTS AND KNOWLEDGE

▶ Language of position
▶ Language of measurement

PRE-ASSESSMENT

Can the child:

▶ use 'highest' and 'lowest' to describe position?
▶ use 'left' and 'right' to describe position?
▶ use 'longer' and 'shorter' to describe measurement?
▶ use 'wider' and 'narrower' to describe measurement?

The story

The characters are playing after lunch. This involves climbing a hill and pretending it is a castle, like the one they are going to visit. Soon it is time to leave, and they return to the bus. The pages can be used to discuss the differences between 'highest' and 'lowest', 'left' and 'right', 'longer' and 'shorter', 'wider' and 'narrower'. They may also provide an opportunity to talk about the games the characters are playing.

Copymaster 35 provides a format for children to record their answers to the questions in the textbook.

Maths content and resources

The textbook pages present real-life situations in which the language of position and measurement might be used. Ideally, children will experience much of this language in practical situations such as PE sessions.

The activities on pages 8 and 9 of Topic Workbook 2 are concerned with 'top', 'bottom', 'left', 'right', 'middle', 'high' and 'low'. Children write the words and draw symbols in the appropriate places.

The cards on Copymaster 58 are for activities using position words. They can be cut and pasted on to Copymaster 57, or the words can be used to label other pictures or children's drawings and models.

On pages 10 and 11 of Topic Workbook 2, children write the measurement words 'long', 'short', 'wide' and 'narrow' to label pictures.

This is followed up on Copymasters 59 and 60, where they draw simple examples of 'longer', 'shorter', 'wider' or 'narrower' objects.

More measurement activities

At this stage, most measurement activities are essentially practical and should have a practical purpose, or be part of a project. Some appropriate activities are listed here.

Children could pour from one container to another, to check different capacities. This need not always involve water. Lentils, split peas or pasta will give reasonable comparisons.

Children could mix drinks to find out how much orange juice and water need to be used to make drinks for six children. This kind of activity will encourage the use of language such as 'empty', 'full' and 'half-full'.

Children should be encouraged to hold objects in their hands and feel the difference in their weights. Their judgements can then be checked with a beam balance. A useful recipe to support this work is for the 'Two-egg cake'. All its ingredients – flour, butter and sugar – have to be balanced against two eggs, on a beam balance. When the ingredients are balanced, they can be mixed.

Challenging children to activities such as building the tallest tower using Multilink, cylinders or straws is a very useful way to encourage the use of comparisons and the language associated with them.

Paper shapes – such as triangles, circles or rectangles – with different areas can be used to build up layers, to make collages or patterns. The larger areas can be placed beneath the smaller ones, so that areas can be compared practically without the need for standard units.

The materials

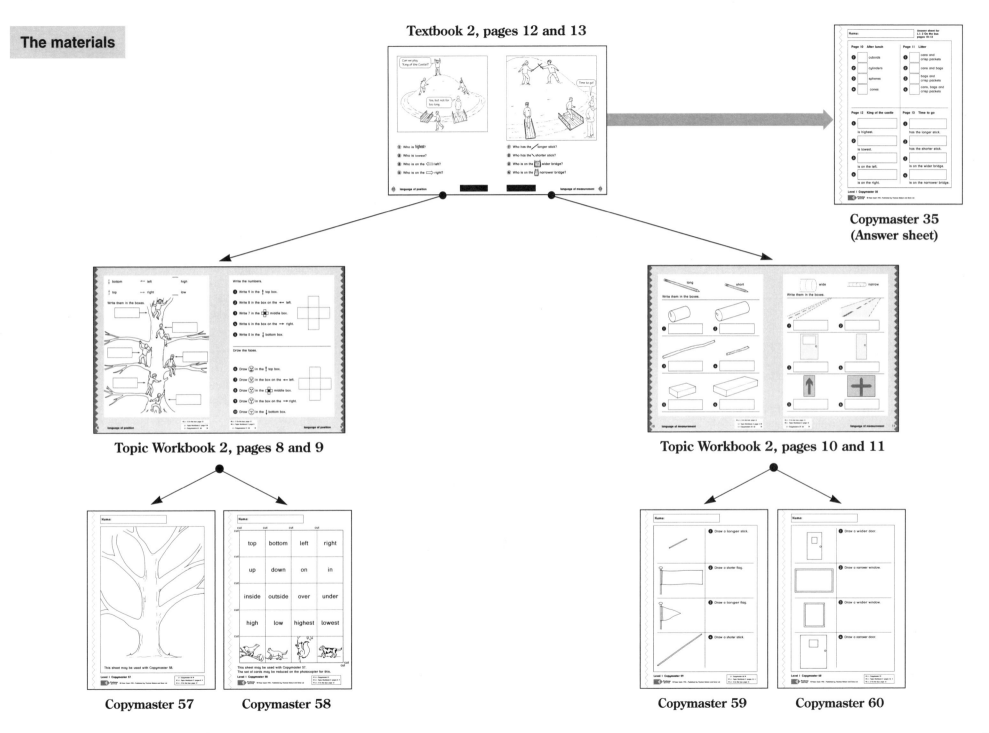

Textbook 2, pages 12 and 13

Copymaster 35
(Answer sheet)

Topic Workbook 2, pages 8 and 9

Topic Workbook 2, pages 10 and 11

Copymaster 57

Copymaster 58

Copymaster 59

Copymaster 60

Approaching the castle

SKILLS, CONCEPTS AND KNOWLEDGE

▶ Copying patterns
▶ Identifying 3D shapes

PRE-ASSESSMENT

Can the child:

▶ identify a brick pattern?
▶ copy a brick pattern?
▶ identify common 3D shapes?

The story

The last two pages show the characters nearing the castle. On the way, they see a brick pattern which they draw. As they arrive at the castle, they see the shapes which make up the component parts of the castle. Page 14 can be used to introduce brick patterns; many different kinds of these may be found in the local area. Page 15 shows how 3D shapes can fit together to make more complex structures.

The top of Copymaster 36 provides space for children to draw the brick pattern on page 14. The lower part gives an answer format for page 15.

Maths content and resources

The activities on pages 12 and 13 of Topic Workbook 2 develop the work on brick patterns from page 14 of the textbook. There are four different patterns for children to continue. These are based on examples from everyday life.

Copymaster 61 provide templates for bricks in two sizes which children can cut out and arrange, to try out patterns. These may be used to support the Topic

Workbook pages and Copymaster 62, which is another worksheet on brick patterns.

Pages 14 and 15 of Topic Workbook 2 look at the 3D shapes which make up the castle and the 2D shapes of the flags.

Copymasters 63 and 64 provide templates for building a cylindrical tower, a box tower, walls and a conical roof.

Building a castle

For this activity you will need Copymasters 63 and 64.

These have been designed to be as simple as possible to cut, paste and fit together, in order to make satisfactory structures.

Cylinder tower

Cut out the shape, bend it round and glue the flap on the inside of the opposite edge.

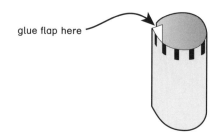

glue flap here

Cuboid tower and castle wall

Before or after cutting out, it is worth scoring the dotted lines. This can be done with a pencil and ruler, to give a sharp fold. Once again, the flap is pasted to the inside of the opposite edge.

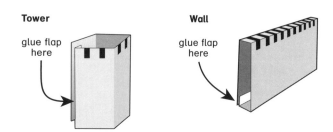

Tower
glue flap here

Wall
glue flap here

Cone roof

This is an optional extra. The cone fits the cylinder tower to form a roof. The flap on the semi-circle can be pasted and attached to the underside of the other straight edge.

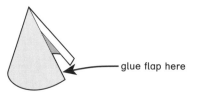

glue flap here

Final construction

All the shapes are open, to allow fingers to be used inside for gluing and taping into position. Walls can be used as they are, or cut to size, in order to fit. The castellation marks may be used as a guide for cutting.

Children can use as many towers and walls as they like to make their own castle. They can be put together on a large sheet of paper, using adhesive tape and glue sticks. Children should be encouraged to adapt the templates to make their own special features, such as gateways.

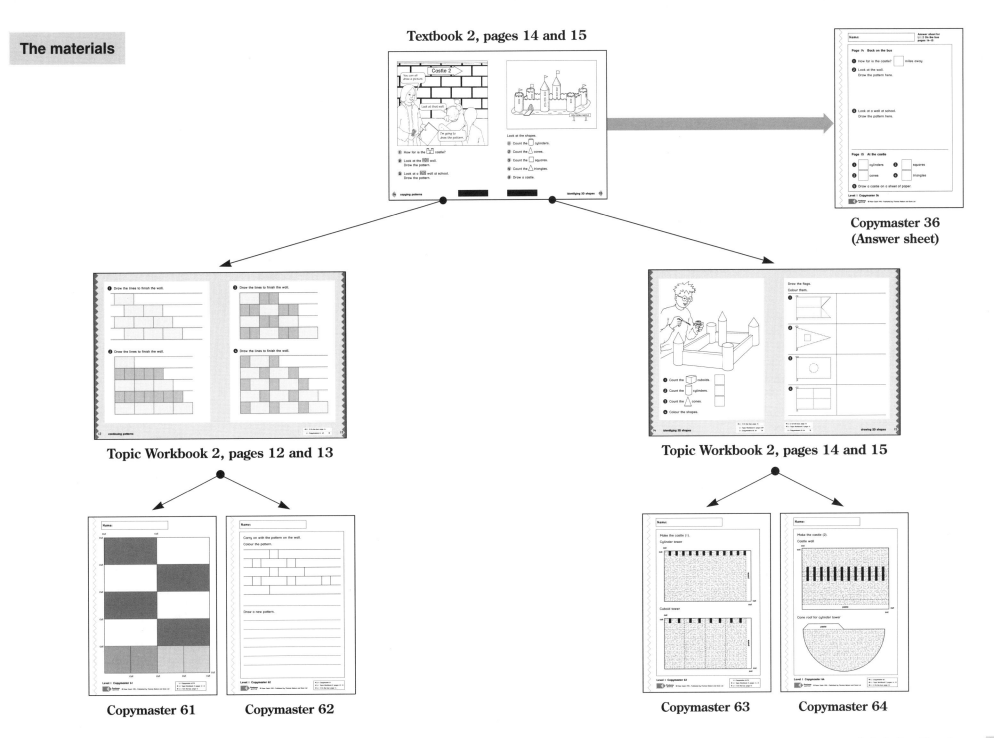

The materials

Textbook 2, pages 14 and 15

Copymaster 36
(Answer sheet)

Topic Workbook 2, pages 12 and 13

Topic Workbook 2, pages 14 and 15

Copymaster 61

Copymaster 62

Copymaster 63

Copymaster 64

L1:3 At the castle

At the castle

SKILLS, CONCEPTS AND KNOWLEDGE

▶ Counting to 10
▶ Reading analogue time
▶ Identifying 2D shapes

PRE-ASSESSMENT

Can the child:

▶ count up to 10 accurately?
▶ tell 'o'clock' times on an analogue clock face?
▶ identify squares, triangles, circles and rectangles?

The story

The characters arrive at the castle courtyard at one o'clock. The teacher issues them with the materials they will need, and they set off to explore. They see the front of the castle lodge, where they stop to draw the shapes they see. The pages can be used as a starting point for discussing what children would take on a school trip, what activities they would do and what they would like to bring back to school.

Copymaster 65 provides a format for children to record their answers to questions in the textbook.

Maths content and resources

The textbook pages revisit counting to 10 and 'o'clock' times on an analogue clock-face. They also introduce 2D shapes as components of buildings.

On page 2 of Number Workbook 3, children can map writing and drawing materials to each character. On page 3, they can count windows, doors and other parts of a building.

Copymasters 71 and 72 are two supporting worksheets providing further practice with mapping work and with subtraction.

On pages 2 and 3 of Topic Workbook 3, children are asked to identify and then draw 2D shapes.

Copymasters 73 and 74 offer more drawing activities, using 2D shapes in patterns and pictures.

Pages 14 and 15 of Topic Workbook 3 support all the work at this level on reading and showing analogue 'o'clock' times. Here children record the times, both by writing them and by drawing the hands on clock faces.

Copymasters 91 and 92 are two supporting worksheets on telling and recording the time.

Copying shapes

For these activities you will need a set of logic blocks and some A4 paper.

It is relatively quick to prepare a simple picture based on the shapes in a set of logic blocks. Black felt pens are ideal for this. Children can be given a photocopy of a picture (as shown on this page), a blank sheet of A4 paper and the logic blocks. They find the appropriate blocks and place them on the picture. There are several examples of the same shape and size in a set, so children can be encouraged to look at alternative colours to suit the picture.

For some children, finding and placing the shapes will be enough. However, the activity can be extended by asking them to transfer the logic blocks on to a fresh sheet of paper, draw round them to reproduce the picture, and colour them to match the shapes they have chosen.

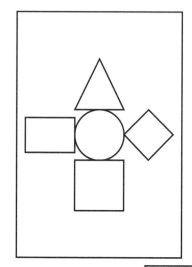

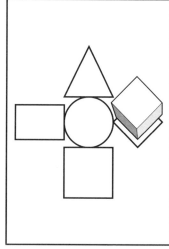

If the original pictures are kept separately, they can become a resource which can be used with different groups. Children may also develop their own ideas for pictures which can be used in the future. Some ideas for simple pictures may be found on Copymaster 74 which can also be used to follow up the activity.

The materials

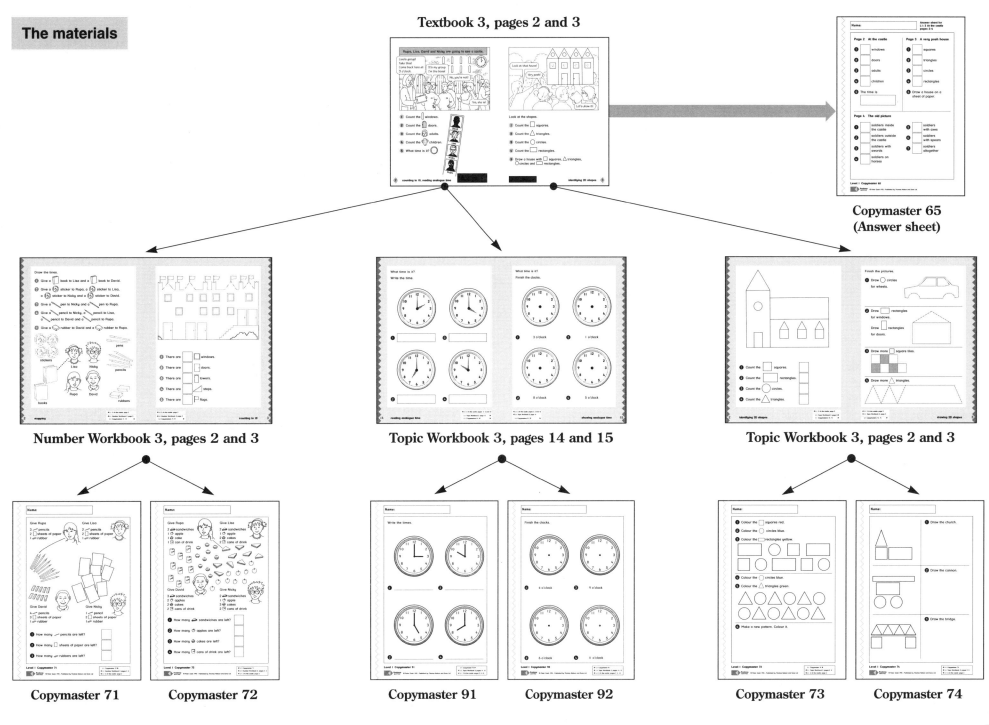

Textbook 3, pages 2 and 3

Copymaster 65 (Answer sheet)

Number Workbook 3, pages 2 and 3

Topic Workbook 3, pages 14 and 15

Topic Workbook 3, pages 2 and 3

Copymaster 71

Copymaster 72

Copymaster 91

Copymaster 92

Copymaster 73

Copymaster 74

Inside the castle

SKILLS, CONCEPTS AND KNOWLEDGE

▶ Counting to 10
▶ Analogue time
▶ Roman numerals

PRE-ASSESSMENT

Can the child:

▶ count up to 10 accurately?
▶ match Roman numerals to numbers?
▶ tell 'o'clock' times on an analogue clock face?

The story

The characters are inside the castle lodge where they find a medieval painting of a siege. Whilst they don't seem to appreciate the style of the painting, they are interested in an old clock with Roman numerals. The characters have not seen one before.

The pages can be used to introduce the idea of maths in pictures. As an additional exercise, children could be asked to find pictures in magazines and catalogues of clocks with different markings.

Copymasters 65 and 66 provide a format for children to record their answers to questions in the textbook.

Maths content and resources

Page 4 of the textbook is supported by further work on pages 4 and 5 of Number Workbook 3. Page 5 depicts a medieval scene, presenting it as a counting situation.

Copymaster 75 is a supporting worksheet with a similar theme.

Page 6 of Number Workbook 3 revisits Roman numerals and page 7 introduces number arrangements. This can be followed up by looking at the number sequences in arrangements of squares, spots and strokes on Copymasters 76 and 77. Children can try to develop their own number systems using different patterns.

Pages 14 and 15 of Topic Workbook 3 and Copymasters 91 and 92 provide more work on telling and showing 'o'clock' times on analogue clock faces.

More numeral activities

For these activities you will need a calculator, magazines, straws, lolly sticks and some card.

Numerals appear in a wide variety of forms in everyday life. One increasingly common form is that used on calculators, video recorders and digital clocks. Children could find these in the classroom by pressing the buttons on a calculator. They could make models of them using straw, lolly sticks or strips of card, which can be stuck down on large sheets of paper.

This can form the beginning of a collection of magazine pictures of different numerals. Roman numerals could be included in the collection, along with any number patterns or arrangements which children make or find themselves.

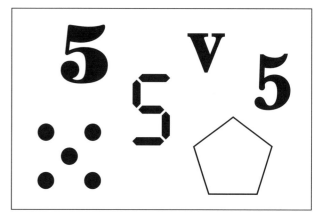

Some children may be able to invent their own number codes, like that on Copymaster 77.

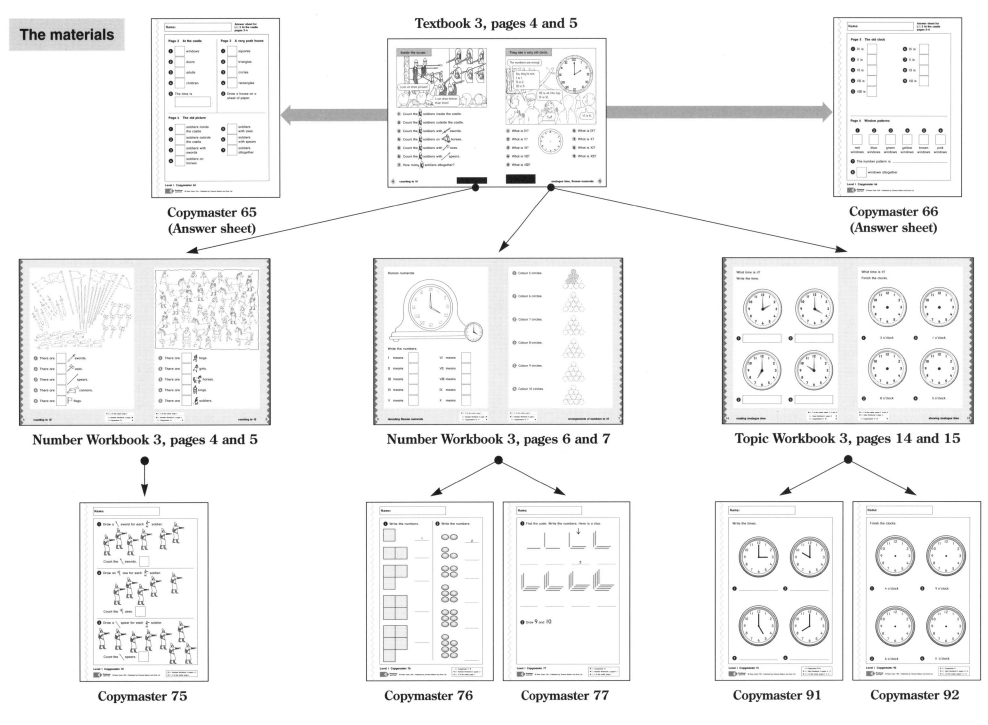

The materials

Copymaster 65
(Answer sheet)

Textbook 3, pages 4 and 5

Copymaster 66
(Answer sheet)

Number Workbook 3, pages 4 and 5

Number Workbook 3, pages 6 and 7

Topic Workbook 3, pages 14 and 15

Copymaster 75

Copymaster 76

Copymaster 77

Copymaster 91

Copymaster 92

The tower

SKILLS, CONCEPTS AND KNOWLEDGE

▶ Number patterns to 10
▶ Counting up, counting down

PRE-ASSESSMENT

Can the child:

▶ find number patterns in arrangements of objects?
▶ use number lines, tracks or steps to count on and back?

The story

The characters find a tower with steps leading up to it. They look at the arrangement of the windows in the tower and then decide to play on the steps. The pages can be used to look at how patterns can generate number sequences. Recurring number sequences are often used to make tile or paving patterns. The numbered steps can be related to real stairs, number lines and number tracks in the playground.

The lower half of Copymaster 66 provides a format for children to record their pattern from page 6 of the textbook. Copymaster 67 provides a format for children to record their answers to the questions on page 7.

Maths content and resources

The work on page 6 of the textbook builds on the work on Roman numerals and number arrangements on page 5. Page 7 asks children to count up and down.

Pages 4 and 5 of Topic Workbook 3 show tile patterns and arrangements of windows. These can generate number sequences. Copymasters 78 and 79

provide worksheets with more examples.

Activities on pages 8 and 9 of Number Workbook 1 continue to use number steps to count up and down. Copymasters 80 and 81 provide two supporting worksheets. Copies of these can be modified to create further worksheets with different numbers on the steps.

More number arrangement activities

Square tiles and squared paper may be used.

Children can be given a number of square tiles and asked to put them together in as many ways as possible. This provides a starting point for discussing similarities and differences between shapes.

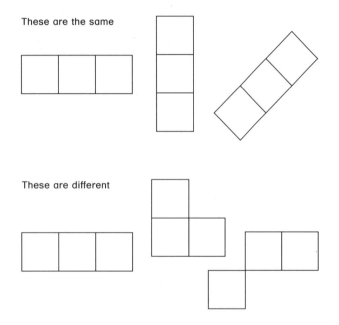

These are the same

These are different

It may be useful, after a while, to introduce a rule that tiles must touch by their edges, not their corners (see *Polyominoes*). Children can be asked to record their different shapes on squared paper.

There are two possible ways of developing this activity:

Odd and even
Children should try to make tile patterns for each of the numbers up to 10. They should attempt to keep the tiles in pairs. This will help them to understand that those numbers that can be arranged in tidy rectangles are even numbers, and those which need a single spare tile are odd.

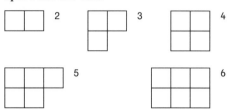

Polyominoes
There is no need to use the term 'polyominoes' to describe the activity. The aim is to try to find all the different arrangements which can be made with a particular number of squares. The squares must fit together so that at least one edge of every square is touching the edge of another square. A shape is counted as different if, when cut out, it cannot be placed exactly on top of another shape, even if it is turned over.

These are the same

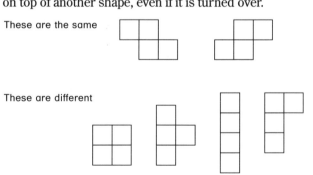

These are different

With three squares, only two different shapes can be made. Five squares can make twelve different shapes, although they can be difficult to find. As an alternative to these activities, equilateral triangles can be used in the same way, and 'triangle' paper can be used for recording.

The materials

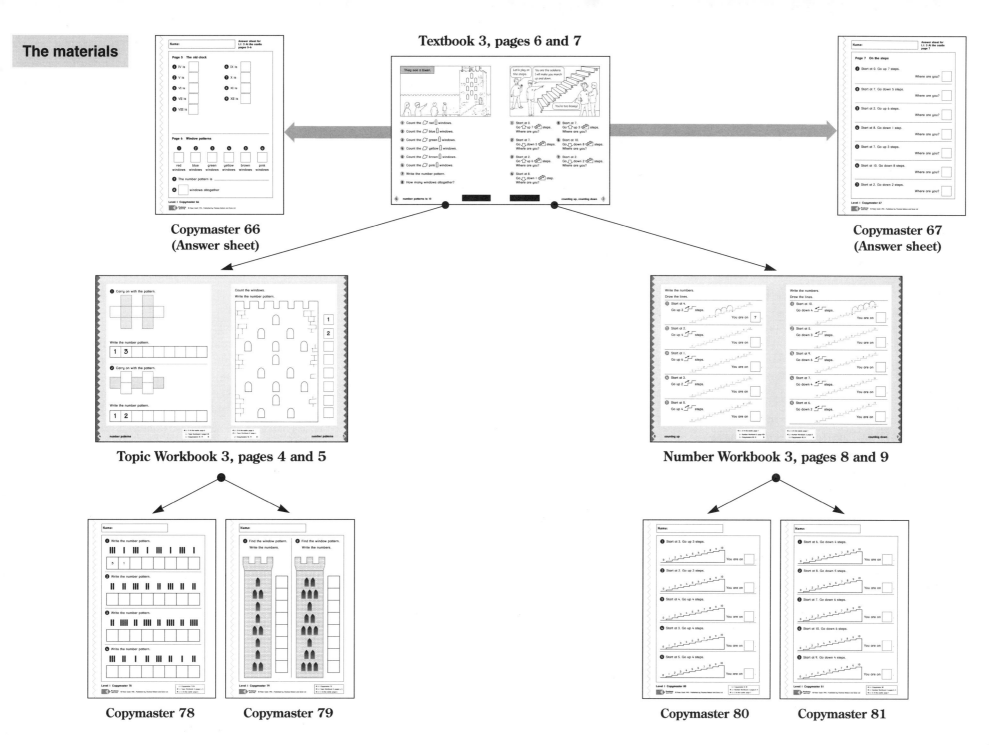

Textbook 3, pages 6 and 7

Copymaster 66
(Answer sheet)

Copymaster 67
(Answer sheet)

Topic Workbook 3, pages 4 and 5

Number Workbook 3, pages 8 and 9

Copymaster 78

Copymaster 79

Copymaster 80

Copymaster 81

The top of the tower

SKILLS, CONCEPTS AND KNOWLEDGE

▶ Language of measurement
▶ Language of position

PRE-ASSESSMENT

Can the child:

▶ use 'highest' and 'lowest' to describe measurement?
▶ use 'longest' and 'shortest' to describe measurement?
▶ use 'over' and 'under' to describe position?
▶ use 'top' and 'bottom' to describe position?

The story

The characters climb to the top of the tower. Lisa reminds them that they have to draw something, so they decide to draw the flags. Afterwards, they go to the gatehouse and the drawbridge to carry on playing. The pages can be used as a basis for designing flags. If children have built the castle at the end of Textbook 2, they can try to make steps or a drawbridge to go with it.

Copymaster 68 provides a format for children to record their answers to questions in the textbook.

Maths content and resources

The textbook pages introduce those words relating to position and measurement which can most easily be used in practical situations.

Pages 6, 8 and 9 of Topic Workbook 3 give more position words for children to write. The measurement words 'long' and 'short' are covered on page 7. Copymaster 83 provides word cards on measurement to support this work. Copymasters 82, 84 and 85 are supporting worksheets which provide further practice with the position words 'higher', 'lower', 'over', 'under', 'top' and 'bottom', and in positioning 2D shapes.

Practical measurement activities

All measurement work at this stage should be approached practically. The cards on Copymaster 83 can be used to help record or display the results of measurement activities. Here are some ideas for developing children's understanding of measurement.

'Long' and 'short' or 'wide' and 'narrow'
Two strips of card of different lengths should be labelled 'long' and 'short'. Cards of different widths can be labelled 'wide' and 'narrow'. As an alternative to strips of card, other shapes or pictures can be used. If three different cards are used, two should be labelled 'longest' and 'shortest', or 'widest' and 'narrowest'. Children can then match the words to objects.

'Heavy' and 'light'
Cards should be labelled with the words 'heavy' and 'light'. Pairs of items of different weights can be used with the cards. For instance, use two balls of plasticine, one weighted with an object, or weight, inside. The two balls will look the same, but children will be able to feel the difference in weight. Alternatively, two identical boxes can be used, one filled with rice, the other packed with crumpled tissues. Children should use their hands, and a beam-balance, to compare 'heavy' and 'light'. Introducing a third item allows the use of 'heaviest' and 'lightest'. Similar comparisons can be tried with 'full' and 'empty', using small plastic bottles, or 'thick' and 'thin', using cylinders made from plasticine.

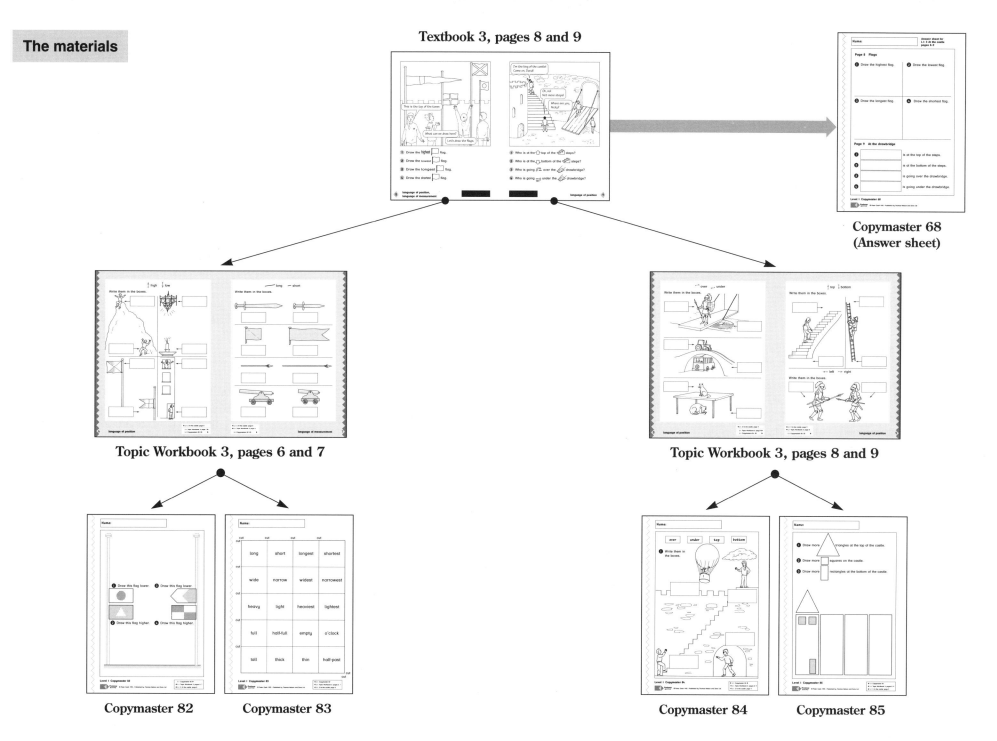

Textbook 3, pages 8 and 9

Copymaster 68
(Answer sheet)

Topic Workbook 3, pages 6 and 7

Topic Workbook 3, pages 8 and 9

Copymaster 82

Copymaster 83

Copymaster 84

Copymaster 85

The cannons

SKILLS, CONCEPTS AND KNOWLEDGE

▶ Identifying 3D shapes
▶ Growing number patterns

PRE-ASSESSMENT

Can the child:

▶ identify 3D shapes in everyday objects?
▶ continue a pictorial number arrangement?

The story

The characters find some cannons and cannonballs near the drawbridge. They tidy up the cannonballs, making a number arrangement. The pages can be used as a basis for looking at how 3D shapes can fit together to make more complex shapes. The arrangement of cannonballs can be tried practically using marbles.

Copymaster 69 provides a format for children to record their answers to questions in the textbook and to draw the cannonball pattern.

Maths content and resources

The textbook pages could introduce more practical work on model making, using 3D shapes. Children could try to make cannons or other models, using cardboard cylinders and old boxes. The work on arranging cannonballs introduces one example of triangular numbers. It is not necessary to pursue this formally, but show more examples of how numbers can grow in this way. Arranging cylinders such as cans will generate the same number sequence (1 + 2 + 3 + 4). In the example on page 11, there are 15 cannonballs. Although this goes beyond numbers up to 10, some children may want to explore the pattern further, keeping a record of the new rows rather than the total number of cannonballs. This may also be a useful way to introduce larger numbers when the children are ready.

The activities on pages 10 and 11 of Topic Workbook 3 show more 3D shapes to identify and to copy.

Copymaster 86 is a supporting worksheet on 3D shape.

Pages 12 and 13 of Topic Workbook 3 look at further ways of generating number sequences from drawings. Page 12 shows a number pattern with steps growing in ones and twos for children to complete. Page 13 shows another way of generating a triangular number sequence, by joining dots. Children may want to explore this further, but beyond five dots the drawing becomes more difficult.

Copymasters 87 and 88 are supporting worksheets. They provide more work on number sequences using patterns.

More number patterns using steps

For these activities, you will need Colour Factor rods, Cuisenaire rods or rods made from interlocking cubes.

Building staircases with real materials is a good way to show regular steps. If Colour Factor or Cuisenaire rods are used, children can record their steps on 1 cm-squared paper. For larger cubes, 2-cm squared paper can be used. This means that children can use the practical materials on the paper itself.

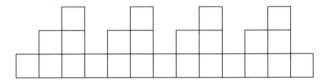

The same materials can be used to show more complex repeating patterns.

Patterns

For this game you will need a large book, Colour Factor rods, Cuisenaire rods or interlocking cubes.

Two children can play. Each one uses a few bricks to make a simple repeating pattern. They are prevented from seeing each other's pattern by a large book propped between them. When they have made their patterns, these are exchanged and they continue with the remaining bricks.

Explain that they need to show a few repeats to make a pattern. For example, one red brick and two blue bricks do not make a pattern in themselves. However, if children are shown one red, two blue, one red, two blue, one red, two blue, they have plenty of clues as to how to continue.

Children can use a variety of apparatus such as Logic blocks, coloured tiles, counters and sorting materials to play this game.

The materials

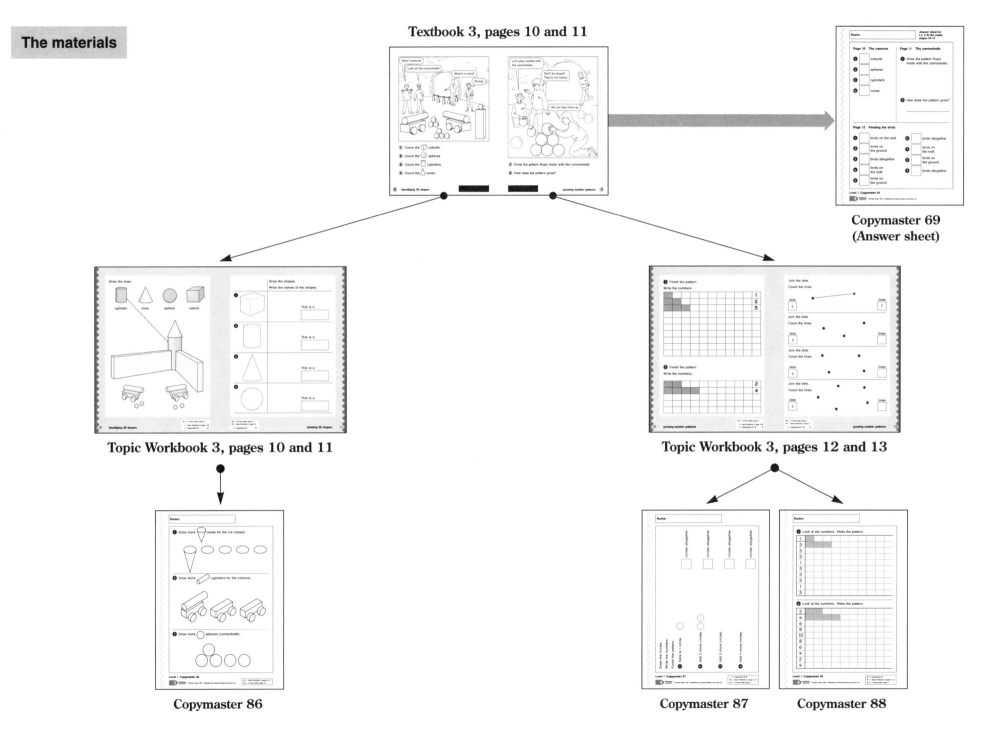

Textbook 3, pages 10 and 11

Copymaster 69
(Answer sheet)

Topic Workbook 3, pages 10 and 11

Topic Workbook 3, pages 12 and 13

Copymaster 86

Copymaster 87

Copymaster 88

On the way to the shop

SKILLS, CONCEPTS AND KNOWLEDGE

▶ Addition to 10
▶ Language of position
▶ Counting to 10
▶ Reading analogue time

PRE-ASSESSMENT

Can the child:

▶ add using picture clues?
▶ identify 'first' and 'last'?
▶ recognise pairs?
▶ tell 'o'clock' times on an analogue clock face?

The story

The children are on their way back to join the rest of the group. They see some pigeons and stop to feed them. Afterwards, they rush to the teacher to ask if they can visit the shop to buy souvenirs.

Copymasters 69 and 70 provide formats for children to record their answers to questions in the textbook.

Maths content and resources

The textbook pages provide some different situations for adding and counting up to 10, for looking at the language of position and for telling the time on an analogue clock face.

Activities on page 10 of Number Workbook 3 provide more addition situations. Page 11 uses the context of birds flying away to show subtraction situations.

There are two more addition and subtraction worksheets on Copymasters 89 and 90.

Pages 4 and 5 of Number Workbook 3 give practice in counting to 10, and are supported by Copymaster 75.

Pages 8 and 9 of Topic Workbook 3 and Copymasters 84 and 85 focus on the language of position.

Pages 14 and 15 of Topic Workbook 3 provide more clock faces for reading and showing analogue time.

Copymasters 91 and 92 provide more practice, and can be adapted to give different examples.

An addition game

For this game you will need two suits of cards (from 1 to 5) from a pack of playing cards.

The two players deal the cards equally. Each has a pile, face down. Together, they take the top card and look at it, without showing the other person. This is to give them time to count the spots, or read the numbers.

At an agreed signal, they put the cards down together, side by side. The first child to say what the numbers add up to wins both cards. These can either be collected and counted up when all the cards have been used, or they can be placed back under the player's pile to be re-used, making the game longer.

The materials

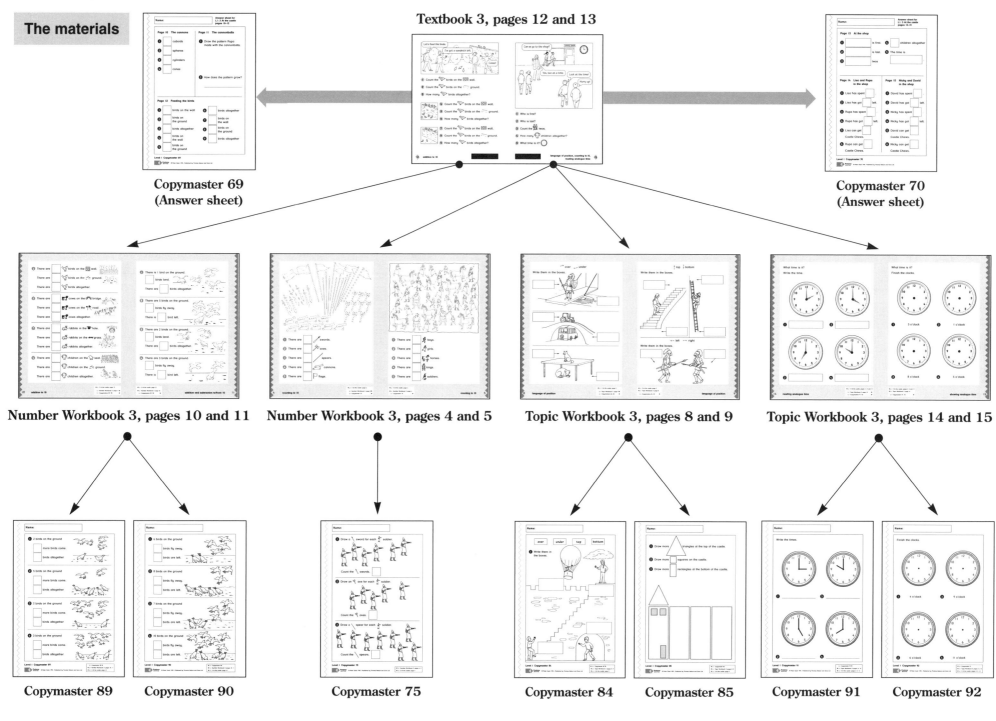

Textbook 3, pages 12 and 13

Copymaster 69 (Answer sheet)

Copymaster 70 (Answer sheet)

Number Workbook 3, pages 10 and 11

Number Workbook 3, pages 4 and 5

Topic Workbook 3, pages 8 and 9

Topic Workbook 3, pages 14 and 15

Copymaster 89

Copymaster 90

Copymaster 75

Copymaster 84

Copymaster 85

Copymaster 91

Copymaster 92

In the shop

SKILLS, CONCEPTS AND KNOWLEDGE

▶ Using money to 10p

PRE-ASSESSMENT

Can the child:
▶ identify a price label?
▶ understand that 'p' means 'pence'?
▶ add two items to find the total cost?
▶ find change from 10p?

The story

The characters visit the castle souvenir shop in pairs. They have 10p each to spend, so they buy small souvenirs. After buying them, they work out how much they have left to spend on sweets.

The pages can be used as a basis for discussing pocket money and shopping, and working out prices. A class shop is ideal for this. However, prices less than 10p can be unrealistic, as there are very few things children can buy in real life for less than 10p. Many children will receive pocket money far in excess of this amount.

Copymaster 70 provides a format for children to record their answers to questions in the textbook.

Maths content and resources

The textbook pages are both about simple shopping situations. The activities on pages 12 to 15 of Number Workbook 3 provide more simple examples of adding amounts and giving change up to 10p.

Copymasters 93 and 94 provide two worksheets for further practice in adding money and giving change. Copymasters 95 and 96 provide cards with coins and price labels up to 10p. These may be cut and pasted, to provide materials for matching and shopping games.

Shopping and using money

For these games you will need Copymasters 95 and 96.

Coin and price matching

The simplest form of this game requires two sets of coin cards, from 1p to 5p. They are mixed up and rearranged, face down, between the players. Each player takes two cards at each turn. If the cards have the same number of coins, the player keeps them. If not, they are returned. They may be returned face up, if the children find it difficult to memorise where they were, otherwise they can be placed face down.

To develop the basic game, different cards can be added as children become comfortable with the rules and with counting coins. Coin cards of higher values, initially 6p and 7p, can be included, until all of the cards up to 10p are in play. Alternatively, a set of price cards from 1p to 5p can be substituted for one of the sets of coin cards. The aim is eventually to play with coins and prices up to 10p.

Can you afford it?

For this game you will need two sets of coin cards (from 1p to 5p) and one set of price cards (from 1p to 10p) from Copymasters 95 and 96.

The cards are split into two piles, the coins in one pile, and the prices in another. Each pile should be shuffled. The first player turns over a price card and a coin card.

If there are enough coins to pay the price, the child keeps the price card and puts the coins back on the bottom of the pile. If there are not enough coins to pay the price, the child keeps the coin card for the next go. The price card remains face up. The next player takes a coin card, to see if they can afford the price, and play continues in the same way.

Children can collect any coin cards they do not use, until they can put two or more together to afford a price card. They do not have to have the exact amount. They can pay more. The winner is the child with the most price cards when they have all been claimed.

Saving up

For this game you will need two sets of coin cards from 1p to 5p, and one set of price cards from 1p to 10p from Copymasters 95 and 96.

This is similar to 'Can you afford it?', but simpler.

The price cards are placed in a line, face up and in order. The coin cards are in a pile, face down. Children take turns to pick up a coin card. If they can use it to buy a price card, they should do so. They can then keep the price card and return the coin card to the bottom of the pack.

They can save up their coin cards to pay for the higher values, but they must save up the exact number of coins before they claim the price card. The winner is the child with the most price cards at the end.

The materials

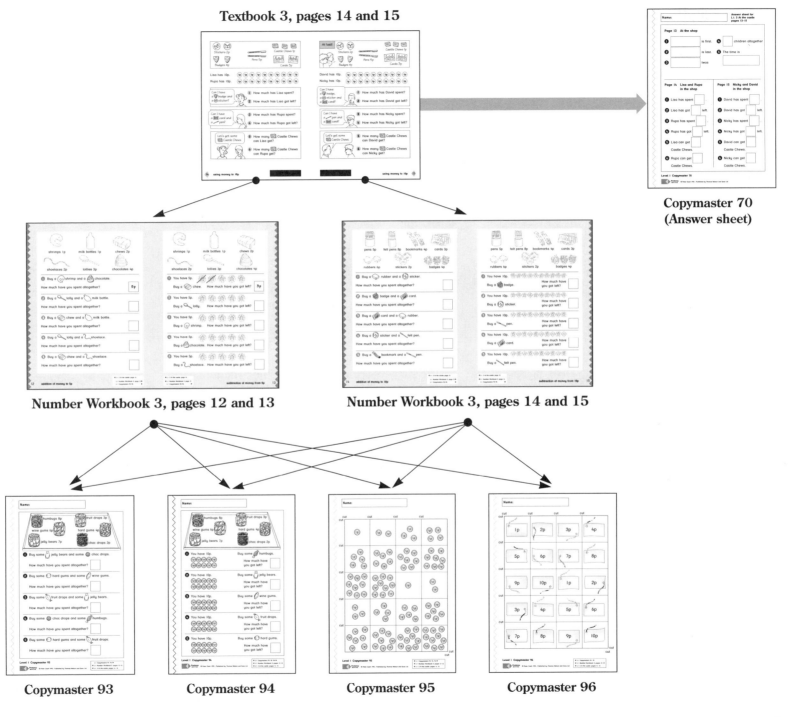

Textbook 3, pages 14 and 15

Copymaster 70
(Answer sheet)

Number Workbook 3, pages 12 and 13

Number Workbook 3, pages 14 and 15

Copymaster 93

Copymaster 94

Copymaster 95

Copymaster 96

L1:4 Goodbye to the castle

PAGES 2 AND 3

Waiting for the bus

SKILLS, CONCEPTS AND KNOWLEDGE

▶ Addition to 10
▶ Identifying 3D shapes
▶ Reading analogue time

PRE-ASSESSMENT

Can the child:

▶ count up to 10 accurately?
▶ sort objects by colour?
▶ identify common 3D shapes?
▶ tell 'half-past' times on an analogue clock face?

The story

The visit is over and the characters are waiting for the bus in the car park. They want to go to the café, to while away the time. The pages can be used to introduce a real traffic survey based on the colours of vehicles passing the school, or even just those in the car park. The 'half-past' position of the long hand on a clock face can be introduced.

Copymaster 97 provides a format for children to record their answers to questions in the textbook.

Maths content and resources

The textbook pages are mainly about counting, to survey colours, vehicles and 3D shapes.

The counting activities on pages 2 and 3 of Number

Workbook 4 are based on vehicles. The first is a small traffic survey, and the second looks at the numbers of wheels on different vehicles.

Copymaster 101 can be cut and pasted to make traffic cards with a vehicle on each card. These may be used to make block graphs for recording the results of traffic surveys.

Pages 2 and 3 of Topic Workbook 4 give further opportunities to identify, count, and write the names of 3D shapes.

Pages 14 and 15 of Topic Workbook 4 deal with analogue time ('o'clock'), as do Copymasters 91 and 92.

Copymasters 120 and 121 extend the work on 'half-past'.

Traffic surveys

Traffic surveys are very useful as they encourage counting and recording numbers. For this activity you will need the cards on Copymaster 101 to make block graphs and tally sheets.

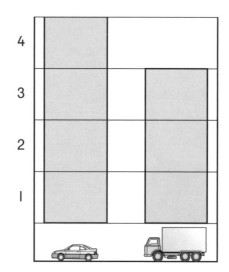

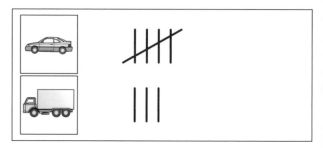

It is always worth asking a specific question, or posing a problem, to begin the survey, for example:

'Are there more red cars than blue cars in the car park?'

'Do more vans than lorries go along the road?'

'Count how many buses pass in the next ten minutes.'

The questions in the survey will depend on traffic density near the school, and the availability of a safe place to watch it from.

Games with traffic cards

For these games you will need cards from Copymaster 101.

Simple games of pairs using memory and matching skills can be devised. These games are based on the cards being arranged face down in front of the children. Players then take two, and try to find pairs which match. Children can add more variety by colouring pairs of cards to be used in the game.

Alternatively, they can take a single card and try to collect all four cards belonging to that set, for example, all the motorbikes. There should be a rule that the first card they take is the set they must collect. If someone else is already collecting that set, they must put the card back.

The materials

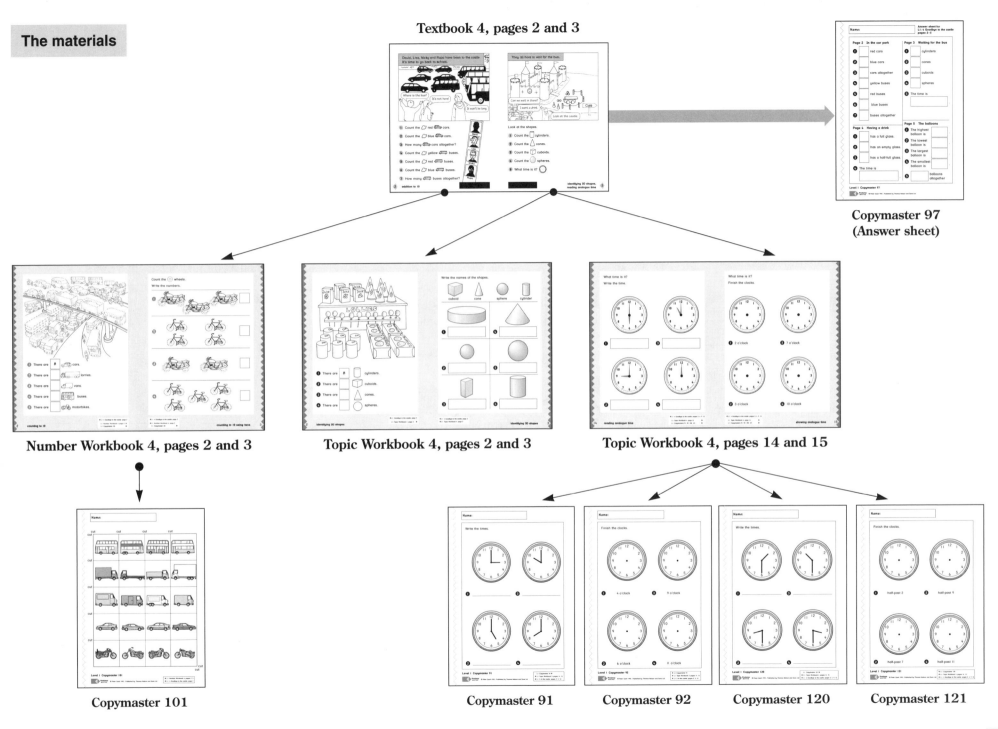

Textbook 4, pages 2 and 3

Copymaster 97 (Answer sheet)

Number Workbook 4, pages 2 and 3

Topic Workbook 4, pages 2 and 3

Topic Workbook 4, pages 14 and 15

Copymaster 101

Copymaster 91

Copymaster 92

Copymaster 120

Copymaster 121

In the café

SKILLS, CONCEPTS AND KNOWLEDGE

▶ Language of measurement
▶ Language of position
▶ Reading analogue time

PRE-ASSESSMENT

Can the child:

▶ use 'full', 'half-full' and 'empty' to describe capacity?
▶ tell 'o'clock' times on an analogue clock face?
▶ use 'highest' and 'lowest' to describe position?
▶ use 'largest' and 'smallest' to describe size?

The story

The children have something to drink in the café while they are waiting for their bus. The time is four o'clock, and there is still no sign of the bus. They ask if they can wait in the play area, and notice some hot air balloons in the distance. The pages can be used alongside practical work on capacity, height and size.

Copymaster 97 provides a format for children to record their answers to questions in the textbook.

Maths content and resources

The textbook pages deal with the language of measurement and position, and with analogue time.

Page 4 of Topic Workbook 4 shows some more situations where children can write 'full', 'half-full' or 'empty'. Boxes of solid objects are used, as well as liquids. Copymaster 102 provides another worksheet on this. Page 5 of Topic Workbook 4 looks at 'heavy' and 'light'.

Page 6 of Topic Workbook 4 asks the children to write 'high' or 'low' to describe position. Page 7 is about identifying the largest and smallest objects. Copymasters 103 and 104 ask children to write and use the words 'highest', 'lowest', 'largest' and 'smallest'.

Pages 14 and 15 of Topic Workbook 4 and Copymasters 91, 92, 120 and 121 provide further practice in telling the time on an analogue clock face.

Capacity activities

For these activities you will need 1-litre or 2-litre plastic bottles, yoghurt pots or plastic cups and a funnel.

Pouring activities are a useful way of looking at 'full', 'empty' and 'half-full'. Drinks containers are commonly 250 ml, 500 ml, 1 litre, 2 litres and 3 litres in capacity. Without knowing the standard units of capacity, children can pour from small containers to larger ones to see how many of the smaller containers it takes to fill a large one. For instance, a 1-litre bottle will half-fill a 2-litre bottle and then be empty itself.

Children can also find out how many cupfuls can be poured from a larger container. For instance, a 1-litre bottle will fill a yoghurt pot about 8 times.

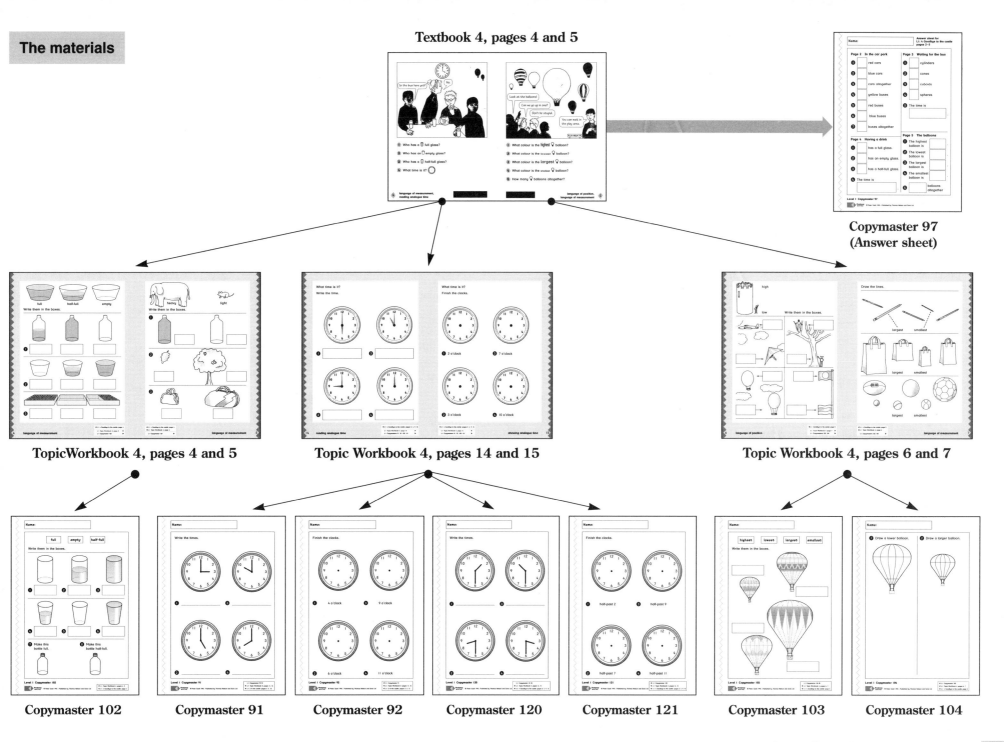

The materials

Textbook 4, pages 4 and 5

Copymaster 97
(Answer sheet)

TopicWorkbook 4, pages 4 and 5

Topic Workbook 4, pages 14 and 15

Topic Workbook 4, pages 6 and 7

Copymaster 102

Copymaster 91

Copymaster 92

Copymaster 120

Copymaster 121

Copymaster 103

Copymaster 104

In the play area

SKILLS, CONCEPTS AND KNOWLEDGE

▶ Using a number line
▶ Continuing patterns

PRE-ASSESSMENT

Can the child:

▶ move along a number line and show the new position?
▶ copy a pattern of tiles?
▶ continue a pattern of tiles?

The story

The children have been allowed to go to the play area to wait for the bus. They find a coloured number line with two big dice and they play a game on it. Then they see a set of tiles, with which they make patterns.

The pages can be used as a basis for discussing the puzzles and activities which children would like to see in a play area. The work on the number line can be developed by devising games, using a similar number line, with bonuses or penalties. The pattern work has been visited before, but with different tiles. Children can also devise their own patterns with square tiles.

Copymaster 98 provides a format for children to record their answers to questions in the textbook. It also provides squares for completing the tile pattern and squares which children can use to devise their own pattern.

Maths content and resources

Page 6 of the textbook is about moving along a number line.

This is supported by further work on page 4 of Number Workbook 4. This covers counting on. Page 5 covers counting back. These pages are based on number lines labelled with the numbers 1 to 10. Number lines may be found or drawn in chalk on the school playground.

Copymaster 105 provides another worksheet on counting on. Copymaster 106 can be adapted to create further number line problems using numbers up to 10.

Page 7 of the textbook shows the children completing a tile pattern.

There are more tile patterns to complete on pages 8 and 9 of Topic Workbook 4. Copymaster 107 provides a worksheet with two more tile patterns. Copymaster 108 provides tile cards which can be photocopied and cut out so that children can move and rotate them.

Tiling activities

For these activities you will need the tiles on Copymaster 108.

Children can also be encouraged to try to devise their own tiles to make patterns.

Moving tiles about, changing their arrangement practically rather than just drawing on to squared paper, should be part of any activity involving patterns.

Encourage the children to try different sorts of tiling arrangements such as lines, crosses and frames.

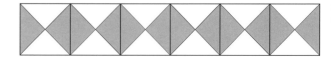

The materials

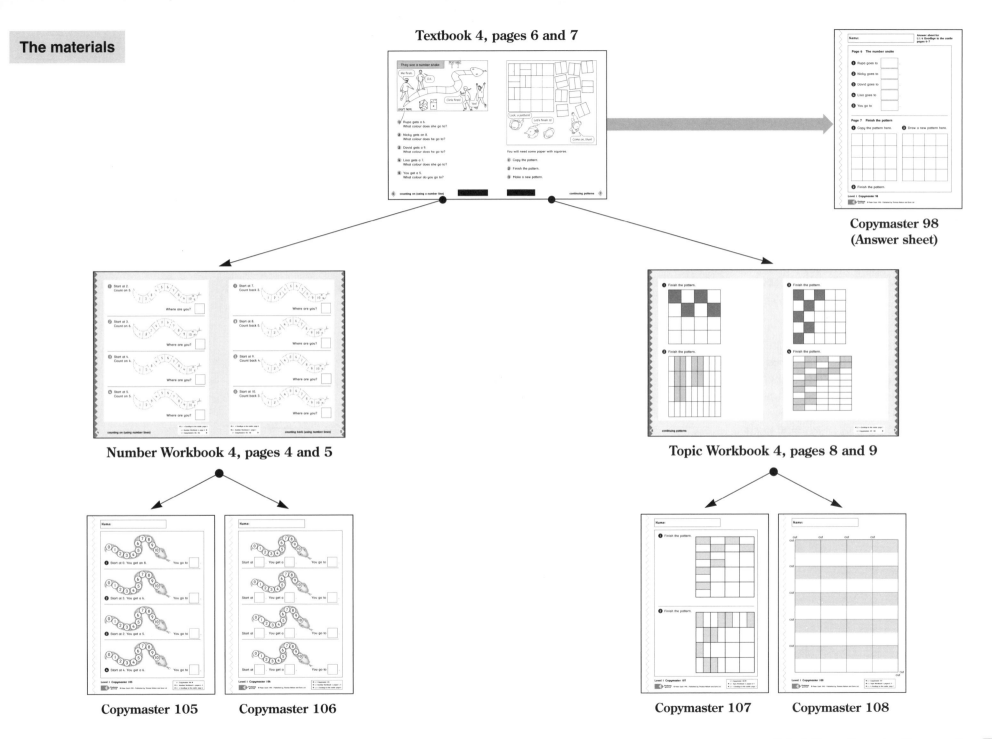

Textbook 4, pages 6 and 7

Copymaster 98
(Answer sheet)

Number Workbook 4, pages 4 and 5

Topic Workbook 4, pages 8 and 9

Copymaster 105

Copymaster 106

Copymaster 107

Copymaster 108

The bus arrives

SKILLS, CONCEPTS AND KNOWLEDGE

▶ Addition to 10
▶ Reading analogue time

PRE-ASSESSMENT

Can the child:

▶ add a list of numbers containing 1 and 2?
▶ tell 'half-past' times on an analogue clock face?

The story

The children have their last game in the play area. This involves running across numbered stepping stones. Then the bus arrives to take them home at half-past four. Page 8 provides opportunities to practise adding lists of small numbers.

Page 9 provides practice in addition to 10.

Copymaster 99 provides a format for children to record their answers to questions in the textbook.

Maths content and resources

The textbook pages give a useful introduction to the addition of lists of numbers and counting to 10, and revisit 'half-past' on analogue clock faces.

Activities on pages 6 and 7 of Number Workbook 4 are also based on stepping stones. For children who find it difficult to add numerals, page 6 has spots to count. Copymaster 109 is a supporting worksheet, and Copymaster 110 can be adapted to provide further worksheets. This will be especially useful for the children who need to use spots.

Pages 8 and 9 of Number Workbook 4 ask children to count the faces at different windows, enabling them to practise counting groups of numbers to add them up. The answers are numbers up to 10. Copymaster 111 is a supporting worksheet.

Pages 14 and 15 of Topic Workbook 4 provide practice in telling the time on analogue clock faces, and are supported by Copymasters 91, 92, 120 and 121.

Classroom stepping stones

For this game you will need Blu-tak and eight sheets of A4 paper labelled with the numbers 1 or 2. For children who are not confident with numerals, large spots can be used.

The sheets of paper can be arranged on the floor and fixed with Blu-tak, to make 'stepping stones' with alternative routes across them.

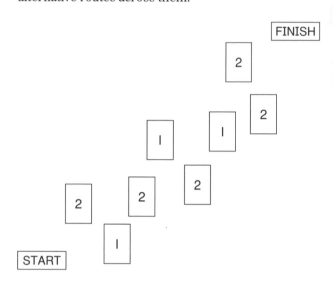

Children can take it in turns to follow a route across the stepping stones. They add up the numbers as they step on them. The winner can be either the person with the highest score or the person with the lowest score.

The arrangement of 'stepping stones' can be simplified by using only five of the numerals. Children can then be asked to find all the possible routes across, and the score for each one.

The materials

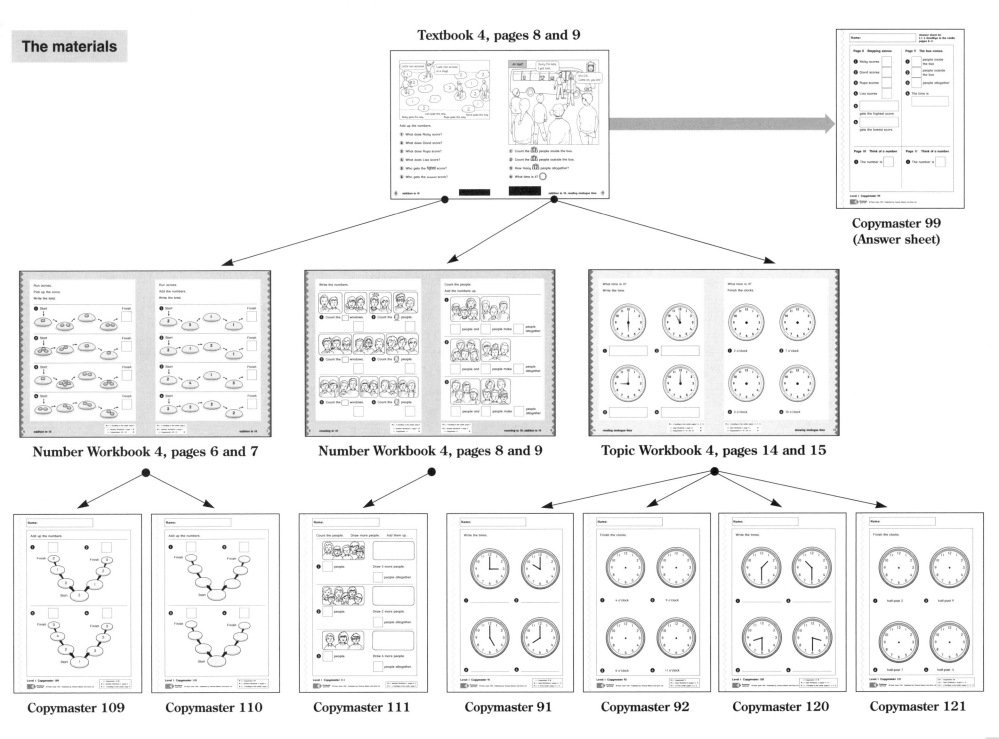

Textbook 4, pages 8 and 9

Copymaster 99 (Answer sheet)

Number Workbook 4, pages 6 and 7

Number Workbook 4, pages 8 and 9

Topic Workbook 4, pages 14 and 15

Copymaster 109

Copymaster 110

Copymaster 111

Copymaster 91

Copymaster 92

Copymaster 120

Copymaster 121

Guessing games

SKILLS, CONCEPTS AND KNOWLEDGE

▶ Larger than
▶ Smaller than

PRE-ASSESSMENT

Can the child:
▶ find a missing number by a process of elimination?

The story

On the bus the characters play a simple guessing game. The teacher thinks of a number below 10, and the children have to ask questions to guess the number. They use words like 'larger' and 'smaller', and try simply guessing. These pages are relatively difficult and it is a good idea to use them in conjunction with guessing games in class, either between children, or between children and teachers.

Copymaster 99 provides a format for children to record their answers to the questions in the textbook.

Maths content and resources

The textbook pages are supported by activities on pages 10 to 13 of Number Workbook 4. These activities consist of 'missing number' problems, using numbers up to 10. Picture clues help children to visualise the situations. Pages 10 and 11 depict coins hidden under a book, to demonstrate missing numbers. Pages 12 and 13 use addition situations with missing numbers, such as: 'If you add this number to 2, you get 5. What is the number?' and 'If you add this number to 3, you get 5. What is the number?' The problems on all these pages can be modelled using practical apparatus such as counters and cubes.

Copymasters 112 to 115 provide more worksheets of this type. The worksheets can be adapted, using correction fluid to erase numbers and spots, and felt-pen to replace them.

Hidden cubes

For this game you will need Multilink or Unifix cubes and a cloth.

A child can be asked to select, and count out, any number of cubes less than 10. For example, they may pick out 5 cubes. The rest of the group may be asked to check the number by counting the cubes. All the cubes are then hidden under the cloth, and another child is asked to remove one of them. The children can then be asked to say how many are left under the cloth. Children may require reminders of the original number and of how many have been taken away. When 4 is suggested, the cloth may be lifted, to confirm that it is correct. The cloth is replaced and the activity is repeated, one cube at a time, until there are none left.

The game can be altered by choosing a different number of cubes to start with. After a while, 2 or more cubes may be removed at a time, or children can choose how many to remove when it is their turn.

This kind of activity gives 'missing numbers' a practical basis, and helps children to develop strategies for finding them.

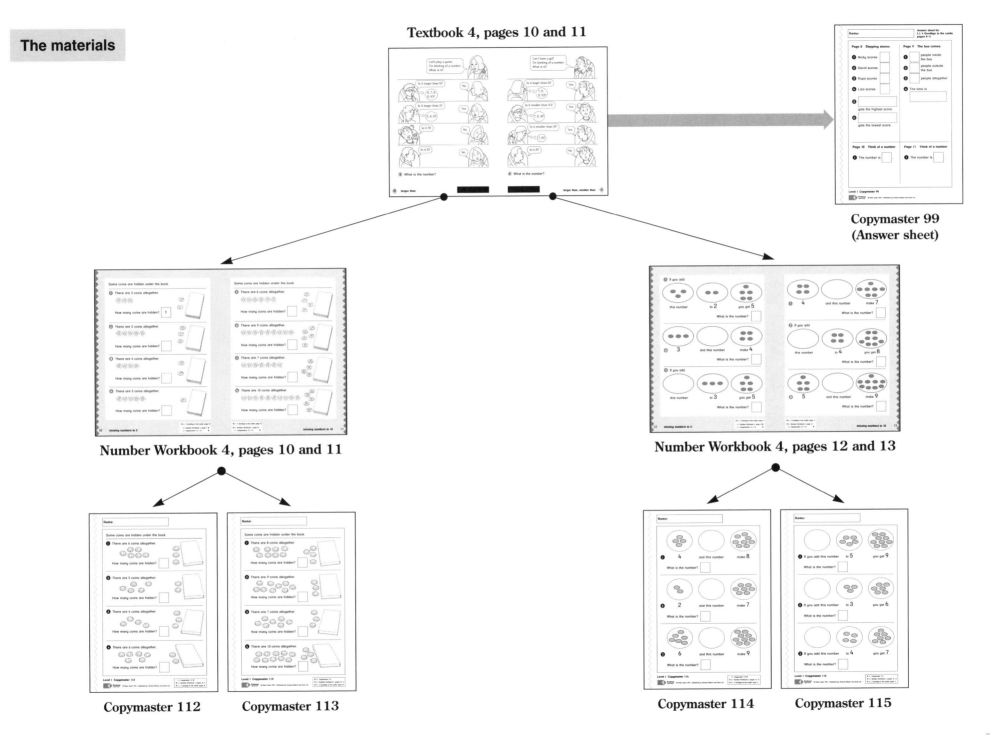

Textbook 4, pages 10 and 11

**Copymaster 99
(Answer sheet)**

Number Workbook 4, pages 10 and 11

Number Workbook 4, pages 12 and 13

Copymaster 112

Copymaster 113

Copymaster 114

Copymaster 115

The last part of the journey

SKILLS, CONCEPTS AND KNOWLEDGE

▶ Language of position
▶ Counting to 10
▶ Addition to 10

PRE-ASSESSMENT

Can the child:

▶ use 'over' and 'under' to describe position?
▶ use 'left' and 'right' to describe position?
▶ use counting to add?

The story

On the final part of the journey home, the characters look out of the windows as the countryside passes by. The pages can be used to look for mathematical situations, such as the positions of objects and number combinations, in the pictures.

Copymaster 100 provides a format for children to record their answers to questions in the textbook.

Maths content and resources

The textbook pages are concerned with the language of position, and the strategy of adding by counting.

Pages 10 and 11 of Topic Workbook 4 provide more pictorial situations for children to label 'over', 'under', 'left' and 'right'.

Activities on pages 14 and 15 of Number Workbook 4 are based on counting animals and people, to practise addition and to see subtraction as being simply a process of counting how many are left. There are two supporting worksheets on Copymasters 116 and 117.

The materials

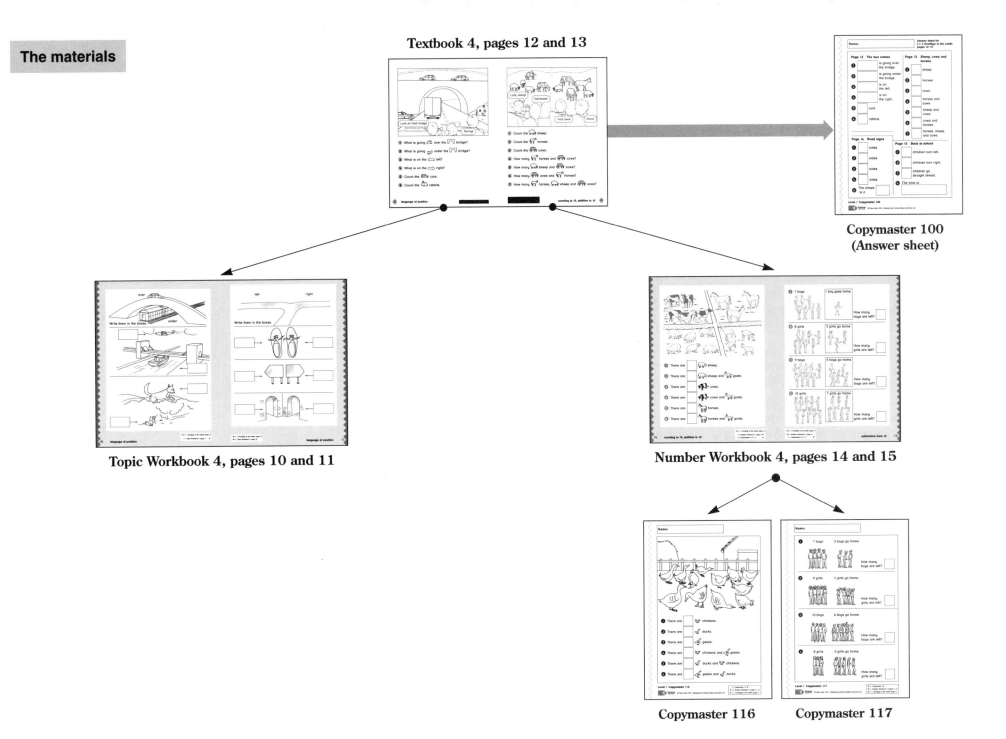

Textbook 4, pages 12 and 13

Copymaster 100
(Answer sheet)

Topic Workbook 4, pages 10 and 11

Number Workbook 4, pages 14 and 15

Copymaster 116   Copymaster 117

Back to school

SKILLS, CONCEPTS AND KNOWLEDGE

▶ Numbers of sides of 2D shapes
▶ Language of position
▶ Reading analogue time

PRE-ASSESSMENT

Can the child:

▶ count the number of sides on a 2D shape?
▶ use 'left' and 'right' to describe direction?
▶ recognise 'half-past' on an analogue clock face?

The story

On the way back to school, the characters see more traffic signs of different shapes and with different numbers of sides. They finally arrive back at school at half-past five. They thank their teacher and set off for home. These pages represent the final part of the story at Level 1. Shapes with more than 4 sides are introduced, and teachers may find it useful to research everyday objects as examples.

Copymaster 100 provides a format for children to record their answers to questions in the textbook.

Maths content and resources

Page 14 covers 2D shapes, and page 15 covers the language of position and analogue time (half-past). These pages summarise much of the work the children have done at Level 1.

Pages 12 and 13 of Topic Workbook 4 develop the work on 2D shapes by focusing on the number of sides. Children count and draw the sides of shapes including irregular pentagons and hexagons. It is not necessary to introduce these names, unless children are ready to use them. It is more important that children should look for examples of shapes with particular numbers of sides in everyday life.

Copymasters 118 and 119 are worksheets providing further practice in counting the sides of shapes and drawing less familiar 2D shapes.

Pages 10 and 11 of Topic Workbook 4 provide further practice in using the language of position.

Pages 14 and 15 of Topic Workbook 4 provide more work on 'o'clock' analogue times. Copymasters 91 and 92 cover analogue time ('o'clock'), and Copymasters 120 and 121 provide work on 'half-past' analogue times.

More activities using irregular shapes

For these activities you will need Geostrips, paper fasteners, straws or used matchsticks, Blu-tak, strips of card and glue sticks.

Children should by now be familiar with regular 2D shapes, and they should have the opportunity of experimenting with irregular shapes and shapes with more than 4 sides.

It is particularly useful to put shapes together using paper fasteners and Geostrips. These shapes can be easily modified. For example, a square can be made into a rhombus:

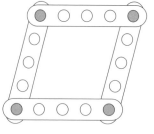

The same can be tried using straws and Blu-tak, or card strips and glue.

Using a combination of lengths for the sides of the shapes will provide some interesting possibilities for new shapes.

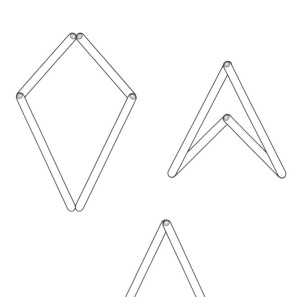

The materials

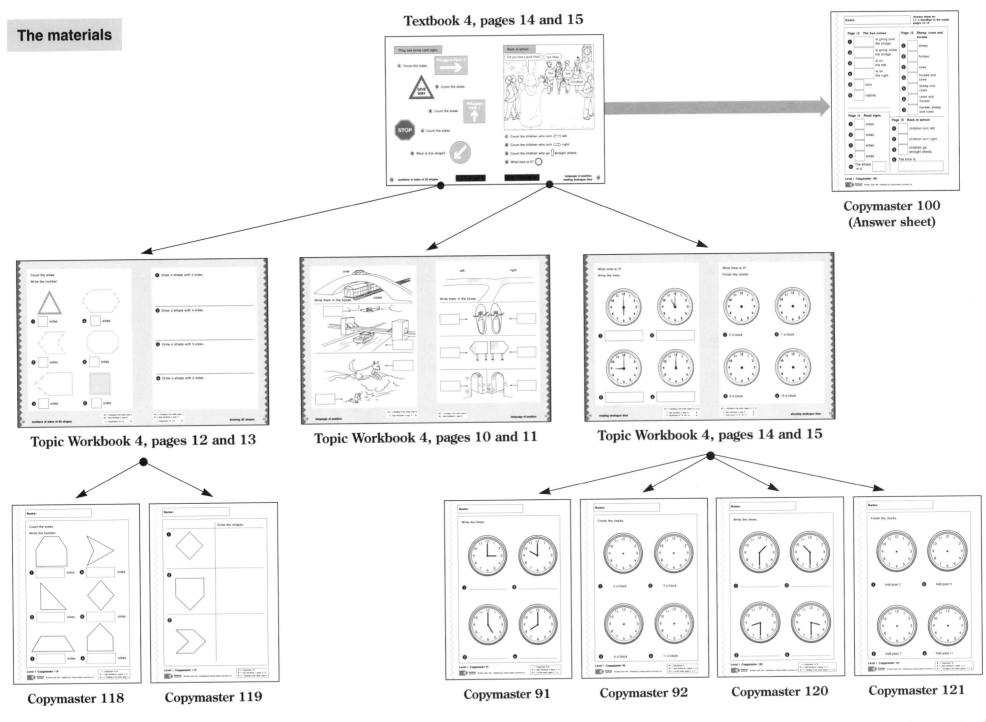

Textbook 4, pages 14 and 15

Copymaster 100 (Answer sheet)

Topic Workbook 4, pages 12 and 13

Topic Workbook 4, pages 10 and 11

Topic Workbook 4, pages 14 and 15

Copymaster 118

Copymaster 119

Copymaster 91

Copymaster 92

Copymaster 120

Copymaster 121

Answers

Textbook 1

PAGE 2
1 4
2 5
3 2
4 3

PAGE 3
1 4
2 3
3 5

PAGE 4
1 3
2 5
3 2
4 8 o'clock

PAGE 5
1 5
2 4
3 3
4 8:00

PAGE 6
1 5
2 9
3 2
4 7

PAGE 7
1 4
2 5
3 2

PAGES 8 AND 9
2 Children should plan, or draw, the short-cut through the tunnel, Short Crescent and Long Way.

PAGE 10
1 the pond
2 the park
3 bricks and cones
4 5

PAGE 11
1 Children's patterns should follow the model.
2 Children's patterns should follow the model but employ a different colour sequence.

PAGE 12
1 2
2 4
3 a blue cuboid

PAGE 13
1 The numbers should run from 1 to 10, and can start at either end of the hopscotch.

PAGE 14
1 Rupa
2 Lisa
3 David
4 Nicky

PAGE 15
1 3
2 4
3 7
4 2
5 9

Number Workbook 1

PAGE 2

1 4
2 3
3 7
4 9
5 8

PAGE 3

6
5
4
3
2

PAGE 4

1 2
2 5
3 7
4 3
5 6

PAGE 5

1
7
9
3
8

PAGE 6

1 Children should draw 4 tennis balls.
2 Children should draw 2 footballs.
3 Children should draw 3 rugby balls.
4 Children should draw 5 golf balls.

PAGE 7

1 Children should colour the picture on the right.
2 Children should colour the picture on the right.
3 Children should colour the picture on the left.

PAGE 8

1 1
2 4
3 4
4 2
5 3

PAGE 9

1 Children should colour the picture on the left.
2 Children should colour the picture on the left.
3 Children should colour the picture on the right.

PAGES 10 AND 11

David's ruler
3 4 5 6 7 9

Lisa's TV control
1   4
  6 7 8

Rupa's calculator
8 9
5 6
  3

Nicky's phone
  2
4
  8 9

PAGE 12

Number square
1 2
  6
7 8 9

Number snake
1 2 4 5 7 8 9 10

PAGE 13

Hopscotch

                              8
1   7   10
             6   9

Number circle
8 7 5 4 3 2 1 (running clockwise)

PAGES 14 AND 15

1 5
2 6
3 7
4 8
5 6
6 9

PAGE 16

I can…
… write the numbers:
7, 9, 8
… write all the numbers to 10:
1 2 3 4 5 6 7 8 9 10

Topic Workbook 1

PAGE 2

1–4 Children should draw the appropriate hands on the clocks.

PAGE 3

1 7 o'clock
2 10 o'clock
3 5 o'clock
4 8 o'clock

PAGE 4

1 08:00
2 05:00
3 01:00
4 09:00
5 02:00
6 03:00

PAGE 5

1 2:00
2 4:00
3 6:00
4 3:00
5 12:00
6 7:00

PAGES 6 AND 7

Children should label circles, triangles, squares and rectangles as appropriate.

PAGE 8

Children should draw a line following Nicky's route.

PAGE 9

Children should draw a line following Rupa's route.

PAGE 10

Children should label
inside – Lisa
inside – Nicky
outside – Rupa
outside – David

PAGE 11

Children should label
over – train
under – bus
left – Rupa
right – David

PAGES 12 AND 13

Children's patterns should follow the model.

PAGE 14

1 cuboid
2 sphere
3 cylinder
4 sphere
5 cylinder
6 cuboid

PAGE 15

Children should use the appropriate colours.

PAGE 16

I can…
… write the name of the shape:
square, triangle, circle
… write these times:
2 o'clock, 10:00

Copymasters for Textbook 1

COPYMASTER 5

1 5 five
2 3 three
3 2 two
4 4 four
5 1 one
6 6 six

COPYMASTER 6

1 7 seven
2 5 five
3 9 nine
4 6 six
5 10 ten
6 8 eight

COPYMASTER 7

1 Children should draw 2 mugs.
2 Children should draw 3 bits of toast.
3 Children should draw 4 oranges.
4 Children should draw 5 packets of crisps.

COPYMASTER 8

1 12:00
2 6:00
3 7:00
4 10:00
5 9:00
6 5:00

COPYMASTER 10

1 Children should draw 6 skulls.
2 Children should draw 7 books.
3 Children should draw 9 aliens.
4 Children should draw 8 disks.

COPYMASTER 11

1 1 o'clock
2 9 o'clock
3 11 o'clock
4 2 o'clock

COPYMASTER 16

1 Children should draw a square.
2 Children should draw a rectangle.
3 Children should draw a triangle.

COPYMASTER 17

Children should write the door numbers,
from 2 to 10.
They should label
2 Nicky's house
5 Rupa's house
7 David's house
9 Lisa's house

COPYMASTERS 18 TO 20

Children should draw the appropriate route.

COPYMASTER 22

Children's patterns should follow the
models.

COPYMASTER 24

1 cylinder
2 cuboid
3 sphere
4 cuboid
5 cylinder
6 cylinder

COPYMASTER 26

1 1 2 3 4 5 6
2 5 6 7 8 9 10
3 1 2 3 4 5 6
4 10 9 8 7 6 5

COPYMASTER 27

1 2
2 3
3 3
4 4
5 4
6 4

COPYMASTER 28

1 5
2 5
3 5
4 6
5 6
6 6

COPYMASTER 29

1 7
2 7
3 7
4 7
5 7
6 7

COPYMASTER 30

1 8
2 8
3 8
4 8
5 8
6 8

COPYMASTER 31

1 9
2 9
3 9
4 9
5 9
6 9

COPYMASTER 32

1 10
2 10
3 10
4 10
5 10
6 10

Textbook 2

PAGE 2

1 5
2 6
3 2
4 4
5 3

PAGE 3

1 10
2 8
3 2
4 3

PAGE 4

1 4
2 6
3 10

PAGE 5

1 8
2 6
3 4
4 2

PAGE 6

1 3
2 5 (including bicycle wheels)
3 2
4 1
5 6 (including the 'no right turn')

PAGE 7

1 the castle
2 the picnic area
3 the town
4 3 (miles)
5 5 (miles)

PAGE 8

1 10
2 7
3 4
4 10
5 10

PAGE 9

1 2
2 3
3 1
4 4
5 1

PAGE 10

1 5
2 6
3 3
4 4

PAGE 11

1 8
2 5
3 7
4 10

PAGE 12

1 Lisa
2 Nicky
3 Rupa
4 David

PAGE 13

1 Rupa
2 Lisa
3 David
4 Nicky

PAGE 14

1 2 (miles)
2 Children's patterns should follow the model.
3 Children's patterns should reflect the brickwork of the wall.

PAGE 15

1 6
2 2
3 2
4 3
5 Children should draw a castle with the appropriate number of towers and flags.

Number Workbook 2

PAGE 2

1 7
2 3
3 5
4 8
5 4

PAGE 3

1 6
2 5
3 3
4 4
5 2

PAGE 4

Children should draw the appropriate lines to pair equivalent sets.

PAGE 5

1 10
2 6
3 4
4 5
5 3

PAGE 6

1 5
2 7
3 8
4 10

PAGE 7

1 4
2 5
3 8
4 7
5 6

PAGE 8

1 7
2 3
3 2
4 1
5 6
6 2
7 1

PAGE 9

1 Children should colour the picture on the right.
2 Children should colour the picture on the left.
3 Children should colour the picture on the right.
4 Children should colour the picture on the left.

PAGE 10

1 4
2 5
3 6
4 3
5 7

PAGE 11

1 9
2 8
3 9
4 8

PAGE 12

1 1
2 1
3 3
4 3
5 4

PAGE 13

1 8
2 6
3 4
4 2
5 0

PAGE 14

1 7
2 6
3 9
4 5
5 8
6 7

PAGE 15

1 4
2 3
3 6
4 3

PAGE 16

I can…
… write the number:
10
… add 4 and 3:
7
… take 2 away from 6:
4

Topic Workbook 2

PAGE 2

1 triangle
2 square
3 rectangle
4 circle
5 circle
6 triangle

PAGE 3

1 circle
2 triangle
3 rectangle
4 square
Children should also draw the appropriate shapes.

PAGE 4

1 the toilet
2 the café
3 the car park

PAGE 5

Children should label
front – Lisa
back – Rupa
left – Nicky
right – David

PAGE 6

1–4 Children should use the appropriate colours.

PAGE 7

1–4 Children should draw the appropriate shapes.

PAGE 8

Children should label
bottom – girl
top – Lisa
left – boy
right – Rupa
high – David
low – Nicky

PAGE 9

1–5

	9	
8	7	6
	5	

6–10

PAGE 10

1 short
2 long
3 long
4 short
5 short
6 long

PAGE 11

1 narrow
2 wide
3 wide
4 narrow
5 narrow
6 wide

PAGES 12 AND 13

1–4 Children's patterns should follow the models.

PAGE 14

1 4
2 5
3 3
4 Children should colour the shapes.

PAGE 15

1–4 Children should draw and colour the appropriate flags.

PAGE 16

I can…
… write the name of the shape:
square, circle, rectangle, triangle

Copymasters for Textbook 2

COPYMASTER 37

1 10
2 3
3 3
4 Children should draw 3 more faces.

COPYMASTER 38

1 Children should draw 6 windows.
2 Children should draw 8 windows.
3 Children should draw 7 wheels.

COPYMASTER 39

1 Children should draw 2 more people.
2 Children should draw 4 more people.
3 Children should draw 3 more people.

COPYMASTER 40

1 Children should draw 6 more coats.
2 3
3 Children should draw 8 more bags.
4 1

COPYMASTER 41

1 4
2 2, 4
3 1, 4, 5
4 2, 3, 5

COPYMASTER 42

1 Children should draw 3 more sweets. 5
2 Children should draw 4 more sweets. 7
3 Children should draw 5 more sweets. 9
4 Children should draw 6 more sweets. 8

COPYMASTER 43

1 Children should cross out 6 sweets. 4
2 Children should cross out 5 sweets. 3
3 Children should cross out 2 sweets. 5
4 Children should cross out 6 sweets. 3

COPYMASTER 44

1 Children should colour the picture on the left.
2 Children should colour the picture on the right.
3 Children should colour the picture on the left.
4 Children should colour the picture on the right.

COPYMASTER 46

1–4 Children should draw the appropriate shapes.

COPYMASTER 47

Children should label
1 straight ahead – the town
2 left – the castle
3 right – the picnic area

COPYMASTER 48

Children should draw a triangle on the left, a circle on the right and a bridge straight ahead.

COPYMASTER 49

1 8
2 4, 8
3 3, 6, 9
4 2, 8, 10

COPYMASTER 50

1 Children should draw 3 more flowers. 8
2 Children should draw 4 more flowers. 7
3 Children should draw 4 more flowers. 10
4 Children should draw 5 more flowers. 9

COPYMASTER 51

1 Children should cross out 3 sandwiches. 5
2 Children should cross out 7 cans of drink. 2
3 Children should cross out 6 cakes. 4
4 Children should cross out 6 packets of crisps. 1

COPYMASTER 53

Children should draw lines to the appropriate shapes.

COPYMASTER 54

1–4 Children should draw the appropriate shapes.

COPYMASTER 55

1 8
2 7
3 7
4 6
5 9

COPYMASTER 56

1 4
2 4
3 2
4 3
Children should draw the appropriate lines.

COPYMASTER 59

1–4 Children should draw objects of the appropriate length.

COPYMASTER 60

1–4 Children should draw objects of the appropriate width.

COPYMASTER 62

Children's patterns should follow the model.

Textbook 3

PAGE 2

1 7
2 4
3 1
4 8
5 1 o'clock

PAGE 3

1 4
2 4
3 4
4 6 (More sophisticated answers would be 7, 8, 9, 10, 11 and 12.)
5 Children should draw a house with the appropriate shapes.

PAGE 4

1 6
2 4
3 5
4 2
5 2
6 3
7 10

PAGE 5

1 4
2 5
3 6
4 7
5 8
6 9
7 10
8 11
9 12

PAGE 6

1 1
2 2
3 1
4 2
5 1
6 2
7 1 2 1 2 1 2
8 9

PAGE 7

1 7
2 2
3 8
4 7
5 10
6 2
7 0

PAGE 8

1 Children should draw a rectangular flag with a diagonal cross.
2 Children should draw a rectangular flag with a vertical cross.
3 Children should draw a triangular flag with a stripe.
4 Children should draw a square flag with a circle in the centre.

PAGE 9

1 Rupa
2 David
3 Lisa
4 Nicky

PAGE 10

1 3
2 8
3 6
4 5

PAGE 11

1   0
   0 0
  0 0 0
2 1 2 3 4 5 6 . . .

PAGE 12

1 2
2 3
3 5
4 4
5 5
6 9
7 4
8 2
9 6

PAGE 13

1 Lisa
2 David
3 3
4 6
5 3 o'clock

PAGE 14

1 6p
2 4p
3 8p
4 2p
5 4
6 2

PAGE 15

1 9p
2 1p
3 8p
4 2p
5 1
6 2

Number Workbook 3

PAGE 2

1–5 Children should draw lines to map the objects to the characters.

PAGE 3

1 10
2 5
3 6
4 7
5 9

PAGE 4

1 7
2 10
3 8
4 9
5 6

PAGE 5

1 8
2 10
3 6
4 3
5 9

PAGE 6

1, 2, 3, 4, 5, 6, 7, 8, 9, 10

PAGE 7

PAGE 8

1 7
2 6
3 7
4 5
5 9

PAGE 9

1 6
2 2
3 3
4 3
5 4

PAGE 10

1 7, 2, 9
2 2, 4, 6
3 1, 4, 5
4 8, 2, 10

PAGE 11

1 3, 4
2 4, 1
3 2, 4
4 2, 1

PAGE 12

1 5p
2 4p
3 3p
4 5p
5 4p

PAGE 13

1 3p
2 2p
3 4p
4 1p
5 3p

PAGE 14

1 8p
2 7p
3 9p
4 10p
5 9p

PAGE 15

1 6p
2 8p
3 5p
4 7p
5 2p

PAGE 16

I can…
… add 4 and 5:
9
… take 2 away from 5:
3
… add 6p to 3p:
9p
… take 4p away from 8p:
4p

Topic Workbook 3

PAGE 2

1 3
2 4 (More sophisticated answers would be 5 or 6.)
3 1
4 4

PAGE 3

1–4 Children should draw the appropriate shapes.

PAGE 4

1 Children's patterns should follow the model.
1 3 1 3 1 3 1 3 1
2 Children's patterns should follow the model.
1 2 1 2 1 2 1 2 1

PAGE 5

1 2 3 1 2 3 1 2

PAGE 6

Children should label
high – David
low – Nicky
high – top flag
low – bottom flag
high – chandelier
low – candle
high – Rupa
low – Lisa

PAGE 7

long   short
short   long
short   long
long   short

PAGE 8

Children should label
over – knight
under – boat
over – tractor
under – bus
over – cat
under – dog

PAGE 9

Children should label
top – top of stairs
bottom – bottom of stairs
top – top of ladder
bottom – bottom of ladder
left – knight
right – knight

PAGE 10

Children should draw lines to the appropriate shapes.

PAGE 11

Children should draw the appropriate shapes.
1 cuboid
2 cylinder
3 cone
4 sphere

PAGE 12

Children's patterns should follow the models.
1 1 2 3 4 5 6 7 8 9 10
2 2 4 6 8 10

PAGE 13

1
3
6
10

PAGE 14

1 2 o'clock
2 7 o'clock
3 4 o'clock
4 10 o'clock

PAGE 15

1–4 Children should draw the appropriate hands on the clocks.

PAGE 16

2 I can…
… carry on with a pattern:
2 3 2 3 2 3 2 3
… write the time:
9 o'clock

Copymasters for Textbook 3

COPYMASTER 71

Children should draw lines to map the objects to the characters.
1 0
2 1
3 6

COPYMASTER 72

Children should draw lines to map the objects to the characters.
1 1
2 5
3 2
4 3

COPYMASTER 73

1–5 Children should use the appropriate colours to make a pattern and then **6** make one of their own.

COPYMASTER 74

1–3 Children should draw the appropriate shapes.

COPYMASTER 75

1 Children should draw 6 swords. 6
2 Children should draw 5 axes. 5
3 Children should draw 8 spears. 8

COPYMASTER 76

1 1 2 3 4 5
2 2 3 4 5 6 7

COPYMASTER 77

1 1 2 3 4 5 6 7 8
2

COPYMASTER 78

1 3 1 3 1 3 1 3 1
2 2 2 3 2 2 3 2 2
3 2 4 2 4 2 4 2 4
4 3 2 1 2 3 2 1 2

COPYMASTER 79

1 1 2 1 1 2 1 1 2
2 2 3 1 2 3 1 2 3

COPYMASTER 80

1 6
2 5
3 8
4 7
5 9

COPYMASTER 81

1 2
2 3
3 1
4 4
5 5

COPYMASTER 82

1–4 Children should draw flags in the appropriate positions.

COPYMASTER 84

Children should label
over – Lisa
under – Nicky
top – Rupa
bottom – David

COPYMASTER 85

1–3 Children should draw shapes in the appropriate positions.

COPYMASTER 86

1–3 Children should draw shapes in the appropriate positions.

COPYMASTER 87

1–4 ○　　　　　　1
　　　○ ○　　　　3
　　　○ ○ ○　　　6
　　　○ ○ ○ ○　10

COPYMASTER 88

1–2 Children should shade according to the number patterns.

COPYMASTER 89

1 4, 6
2 2, 7
3 6, 8
4 6, 9

COPYMASTER 90

1 4, 2
2 3, 5
3 4, 3
4 6, 4

COPYMASTER 91

1 3 o'clock
2 5 o'clock
3 10 o'clock
4 8 o'clock

COPYMASTER 92

1–4 Children should draw the appropriate hands on the clocks.

COPYMASTER 93

1 9p
2 10p
3 10p
4 10p
5 7p

COPYMASTER 94

1 2p
2 3p
3 4p
4 7p
5 6p

Textbook 4

PAGE 2

1 3
2 2
3 5
4 1
5 3
6 1
7 5

PAGE 3

1 9
2 8
3 7
4 5
5 half-past 3

PAGE 4

1 Rupa
2 Lisa
3 David
4 4 o'clock

PAGE 5

1 red
2 blue
3 green
4 yellow
5 7

PAGE 6

1 black
2 brown
3 orange
4 grey
5 purple

PAGE 7

1–3 Children's patterns should follow the model.

PAGE 8

1 8
2 9
3 7
4 6
5 David
6 Lisa

PAGE 9

1 3
2 7
3 10
4 half-past 4

PAGE 10

1 4

PAGE 11

1 7

PAGE 12

1 cars
2 a lorry
3 a police car
4 rabbits
5 3
6 5

PAGE 13

1 5
2 2
3 3
4 5
5 8
6 5
7 10

PAGE 14

1 4
2 3
3 4
4 8
5 circle

PAGE 15

1 3
2 1
3 4
4 half-past 5

Number Workbook 4

PAGE 2

1 8
2 7
3 10
4 6
5 9

PAGE 3

1 6
2 8
3 4
4 10

PAGE 4

1 7
2 9
3 8
4 10

PAGE 5

1 4
2 3
3 5
4 7

PAGE 6

1 6
2 7
3 10
4 8

PAGE 7

1 7
2 6
3 10
4 8

PAGE 8

1 4
2 8
3 3
4 9
5 5
6 10

PAGE 9

1 4, 3, 7
2 5, 3, 8
3 4, 5, 9

PAGE 10

1 1
2 2
3 2
4 4

PAGE 11

1 2
2 4
3 3
4 5

PAGE 12

1 3
2 1
3 2

PAGE 13

1 3
2 4
3 4

PAGE 14

1 6
2 10
3 5
4 9
5 3
6 7

PAGE 15

1 6
2 5
3 4
4 3

PAGE 16

I can…
… add 3 and 5:
8
… take 4 from 9:
5
… find the missing number:
4

Topic Workbook 4

PAGE 2

1 8
2 9
3 6
4 10

PAGE 3

1 cylinder
2 sphere
3 cuboid
4 cone
5 sphere
6 cylinder

PAGE 4

1 half-full – full – empty
2 empty – half-full – full
3 full – empty – half-full

PAGE 5

1 heavy light
2 light heavy
3 light heavy

PAGE 6

Children should label
high – aeroplane
low – hang-glider
high – balloon
low – balloon
high – Nicky
low – Lisa
high – flag
low – flag

PAGE 7

1 Children should draw lines to the appropriate objects.

PAGES 8 AND 9

1–4 Children's patterns should follow the models.

PAGE 10

Children should label
over – car
under – train
over – aeroplane
under – boat
over – fox
under – rabbit

PAGE 11

Children should label left and right as appropriate.

PAGE 12

1 3
2 6
3 5
4 6
5 8
6 4

PAGE 13

1–4 Children should draw the appropriate shapes.

PAGE 14

1 6 o'clock
2 9 o'clock
3 11 o'clock
4 12 o'clock

PAGE 15

1–4 Children should draw the appropriate hands on the clocks.

PAGE 16

I can…
… show 4 o'clock.
Children should draw the appropriate hands on the clock.
… finish a pattern.
Children's patterns should follow the model.
… draw a shape with 4 sides.
The shape need not be a rectangle or a square.

Copymasters for Textbook 4

COPYMASTER 102

1 empty
2 half-full
3 full
4 half-full
5 empty
6 full
7–8 Children should complete the drawings.

COPYMASTER 103

Children should label the balloons appropriately.

COPYMASTER 104

1–2 Children should draw balloons in the appropriate positions.

COPYMASTER 105

1 8
2 9
3 7
4 10

COPYMASTER 107

1–2 Children's patterns should follow the models.

COPYMASTER 109

1 8
2 8
3 10
4 9

COPYMASTER 111

1 Children should draw 5 more people.
   5, 10
2 Children should draw 2 more people. 6, 8
3 Children should draw 6 more people. 3, 9

COPYMASTER 112

1 3
2 3
3 1
4 4

COPYMASTER 113

1 4
2 6
3 4
4 6

COPYMASTER 114

1 4
2 5
3 3

COPYMASTER 115

1 4
2 3
3 3

COPYMASTER 116

1 5
2 4
3 3
4 8
5 9
6 7

COPYMASTER 117

1 4
2 5
3 4
4 3

COPYMASTER 118

1 6
2 3
3 4
4 4
5 4
6 5

COPYMASTER 119

1–3 Children should draw the appropriate shapes.

COPYMASTER 120

1 half-past 1
2 half-past 8
3 half-past 10
4 half-past 3

COPYMASTER 121

Children should draw the appropriate hands on the clocks.

Key vocabulary

These lists provide a summary of vocabulary used in the Level 1 textbooks.

Level 1 – Vocabulary of mathematics

Number

count
number(s)
score
how many
(altogether)
add (up)
how much (many) ...
  left
takes

Shape and space

pattern
shape(s)
side(s)
circle
square(s)
rectangle(s)
triangle(s)
sphere(s)
cuboid(s)
cylinder(s)
cone(s)

Measures

long
longer
longest
shortest
largest
smallest

larger than
smaller than
wider
narrower
full
empty
half-full
heavy

What time is it?
o'clock

Position/direction

highest
lowest
top
bottom
front
back
in(side)
out(side)
on
over

under
up
down
order
first
second
third
fourth
last
left
right
straight ahead

NB Instructional language

Draw ...
Copy ...
Make ...
Finish ...
Write ...

Level 1 – General vocabulary

a
a
across
adults
all
an
and
apples
are
area
arrows
at
axes

b
back
badge(s)
bag(s)
balloon(s)
be
been
belts
better
birds
bits
blue
book(s)
boring
boss

bossy
boys
bridge
brown
bus
buses
but

c
cakes
calls
can
cannonballs
cannons
cans
card(s)
cars
castle
chews
children
clock
close
colour
come
cones
cooee
cows
crisp(s)
cut

d
David
David's
desk
did
disks
do
does
don't
doors
draw
drawbridge
drink

e
eat

f
feed
find
flag(s)
for

g
game
get(s)
girls

glass
go
goes
good
goodbye
got
going
green
ground
group
grow

h
has
have
he
hello
here
hopscotch
horses
house
how
hurry

i
I
ice cream
I'm

in
is
it
it's
I've

j
–

k
king

l
late
left
let's
level
likes
Lisa
Lisa's
litter
live
look
lost
lot

m
make
made
map
marbles
march
me
mess
milk bottles
mmm
mooo
more
mugs
my

n
need
new
next
Nicky
Nicky's
no
not

o
of
off

on
old
on
one
out
O.K.

p
packet(s)
page
paper
park
pencils
pen(s)
people
picnic
picture
pink
play
polygon
posh
put

q
–

r
rabbits
red
road
read
ribbons
right
room
rubbers
run
Rupa
Rupa's

s
sandwich
sandwiches
school
seat(s)
see
she
sheep
shirts
shop
short
signs
slug
snakes
socks
soldiers

some
sorry
spears
start
steps
stick
sticker(s)
stupid
sweets
swords

t
take
than
that
the
them
then
there
they
they're
thinking
this
tidy
tiles
to
toast
too
tower

town
train
trip
tunnel
turn
two(s)

u
–

v
very

w
wait
wall
want
way
we
we've
what
what's
wheels
when
where
who

will
windows
with
won't
wow
wrong

x
–

y
yellow
yes
yet
you
you're
your

z
–